TAKE IT BY FORCE!

How To Possess Your Possessions

LEKE SANUSI

Oraword Publications UK

Copyright © 2006 LEKE SANUSI. All Rights Reserved.

No part of this book may be reproduced, stored in a retrieval system, or transmitted by any means without the written permission of the author.

First published in the United Kingdom by Oraword Publishers UK
June 2006

ISBN: 0-9547416-1-7

Printed by supreme**printers**.com

Cover design by: Chosengraphics.com

All scriptures in this book are from the King James Version of the Bible, unless otherwise indicated.

For further information, contact the author:

Oraword Publications UK
146 Iron Mill Lane
Crayford
Kent, DA1 4RX
E-mail: leke@sanusi.fsnet.co.uk

Or

The Redeemed Christian Church of God
Victory House, London
5, Congreve Street
London SE17 1TJ
Tel: +44 207 252 7522
E-mail: lekesanusi@rccgvictoryhouse.com

DEDICATION

I dedicate this book to my Lord Jesus Christ who continues to make me a weapon of war, a battle axe and a sharp threshing instrument with teeth. By His grace I am saved and by His grace I shall remain saved for His eternal glory. Thank you my Saviour. Unto You be all the glory, honour and praise forever.

TABLE OF CONTENTS

Dedication.. iii
Acknowledgments.. v

Why I wrote this Book... 6

Chapter One
KNOW YOUR STRENGTH 9

Chapter Two
SWIM IN THE RIVER OF GRACE 15

Chapter Three
I WILL NOT LET YOU GO 23

Chapter Four
I SHALL GO VERY FAR 33

Chapter Five
MY HAIR WILL GROW AGAIN 44

Chapter Six
I WILL RECOVER ALL (OPERATION ZIGLAG) 58

Chapter Seven
SHOOT THE ARROW OF DELIVERANCE 72

Chapter Eight
BREAKING BARRIERS TO BREAKTHROUGHS 83

Chapter Nine
TAKE IT FORCEFULLY IN HIS NAME 93

Chapter Ten
UPROOTING THE GATE OF THE ENEMY 104

Appendix 117

ACKNOWLEDGEMENTS

I thank the Almighty God for giving me the inspiration to write this book.

I am grateful to all my spiritual Fathers who continue to mentor me in the long walk with God. I thank Pastor E.A. Adeboye, my General Overseer, his wife, Pastor (Mrs) Folu Adeboye, (Mummy G.O), a true mother in Christ; Rev. (Dr) Moses Aransiola and Pastor Brown Oyitso. God will satisfy you all with long life. I also thank all Pastors and Ministers who give me the opportunity to share the Good News with their congregations. You will all be great in Jesus' name.

I appreciate and celebrate my darling wife, my jewel of inestimable value who intercedes for me without ceasing and takes care of the home as I answer the call of God from one end of the Atlantic to the other. May the Lord bless and keep you.

I thank our miracle boys, Tobi and Tomi who now understand when Daddy wants to be alone and co-operate fully at those times. May you seek God early and stick to Him forever.

To Deacon Wale Olatoyinbo and Miss Tope Oyelakin, I say thank you for your efforts in proofreading the manuscripts under a tight deadline. God bless you.

And to the entire membership of The Redeemed Christian Church of God, Victory House, London, I say thank you for giving me the privilege of being your Pastor and for praying for me without ceasing. Victory is yours permanently in Jesus' name.

WHY I WROTE THIS BOOK

In Matthew 11:12, the Bible says: *"And from the days of John the Baptist until now, the Kingdom of heaven suffereth violence and the violent take it by force."* This scripture has opened my eyes to certain spiritual truths which form the bedrock of the principles I have shared in this book.

I understand from the combined study of this scripture with other passages in the Word of God that certain rights belong to the Kingdom citizen, that is, a born again Christian. I call them 'Kingdom Blessings'. **Ephesians 1:3** makes it clear that God has blessed us with all spiritual blessings in heavenly places in Christ. However, these blessings and rights are under constant violent attacks by the resisting and hindering forces of darkness. (They are 'suffering violence'). In order to possess what rightly belongs to us as believers, we must be violent. That is the essence of spiritual warfare: It is a 'wrestling match'. **Ephesians 6:12**.

Christ's death and resurrection gave us the key to access our kingdom rights. But as you try to apply the key, you meet with resistance from Lucifer and his agents who are still very much active for now. That is why being born again does not mean the end of obstacles, problems and mountains. But of course, being born again guarantees you the ultimate victory if you fight the *'good fight of faith'*. The fact that the Bible calls you the 'violent' means that there is a definite irresistible force at work in your life to overcome when you are born again. Every believer is in the battlefront and our weapons of warfare are not canal, they are *"mighty through God to the pulling down of strongholds,"* (2 Corinthians 10:4).

This book shows you your kingdom rights and possessions; the fierce opposition to them from the powers of darkness; the strategies to prepare you for battle and then the prayers that constitute your weapons of warfare for sure and certain victory.

To turn this book to your testimony, you must surrender your life to Jesus, commit yourself to a lifestyle of uncompromising holiness; read and understand the messages and principles; study and meditate on the scriptures; pray the prayer arrows with aggression and fasting and most importantly, give God violent and unlimited praise and worship.

I will read your testimony very soon in Jesus' name.

Leke Sanusi

London. June 2006

CHAPTER ONE
KNOW YOUR STRENGTH

"...but the people that do know their God shall be strong, and do exploits" Daniel 11:32

When you know your God, you will know your goal. When you know your goal, you are on your way to getting your gold.

An increasing knowledge of God is the best way to keep your destiny in shape. When you increase in the knowledge of God, you will increase in His wisdom, His Spirit and His favour. Paul's greatest desire was to know God more. He declared, *"That I may know Him, and the power of His resurrection, and the fellowship of His sufferings, being made conformable unto His death"* **(Philippians 3:10).** The desire of every believer must be to want to be like Jesus.

To take hold of your destiny by force, you need strength. The strength you need is not human strength. You need the supernatural strength of God and that comes through intimate knowledge of God. **Psalm 28:7-8.** *"The Lord is my strength and my shield; my heart trusted in him, and I am helped: therefore my heart greatly rejoiceth; and with my song will I praise him. The Lord is their strength, and he is the saving strength of his anointed."*

Jesus Christ endorsed a lady's hunger to know Him more. This was in spite of her sister's apparently justifiable complaint of lack of help from her sibling in caring for the guests which included Jesus. Jesus said the sister complained against had made the right choice. See **Luke 10:38-42**. You will make the right choice this year in Jesus' name.

General Douglas McArthur, a military strategist said one of the important requirements for military victory is to know your strength. This comes before knowing the enemy, even though that is also important. For believers, the Lord is our strength in spiritual warfare. In **Psalm 27**, David believed that if he could only dwell in the house of the Lord and keep enjoying His fellowship and growing in the beautiful knowledge of Him, all his enemies will be in trouble. David was right because he never lost any battle in his lifetime. His enemies always stumbled and fell. That will be the portion of your enemies in Jesus' name. But you must do as David did: hunger and thirst for God. *"…but the people that do know their God shall be strong, and do exploits"* **Daniel 11:32**.

A daily walk with God, deliberate lifestyle of holiness, voracious study of the word of God and uninterrupted dynamic prayer life will facilitate an increased knowledge of God.

TESTIMONY: Pastor E. A. Adeboye prescribed in his book *"Open Heavens Devotional"* that we pray Paul's prayers in **Ephesians 1:16-19** and **Colossians 1:9-10** for three months. I studied those scriptures carefully through different translations. I came up with several powerful prayer points from the scriptures. I prayed them daily for thirty days. My spiritual life took a giant leap and my heavens opened like never before. Now I am determined to pray those prayers (set out below) daily for three months and I strongly recommend you do the same. Now, this is your first master-key for taking it by force: KNOW YOUR STRENGTH. Go ahead and apply it.

SCRIPTURES FOR MEDITATION AND PRAYER

Daniel 11:32, *"And such as do wickedly against the covenant shall he corrupt by flatteries: but the people that do know their God shall be strong, and do exploits."*

Philippians 3:10, *"That I may know him, and the power of his resurrection, and the fellowship of his sufferings, being made conformable unto his death;"*

Ephesians 1:16-19, *"Cease not to give thanks for you, making mention of you in my prayers; [17] That the God of our Lord Jesus Christ, the Father of glory, may give unto you the spirit of wisdom and revelation in the knowledge of him:* [18] **The eyes of your understanding being enlightened; that ye may know what is the hope of his calling, and what the riches of the glory of his inheritance in the saints,** [19] **And what is the exceeding greatness of his power to us-ward who believe, according to the working of his mighty power,"**

Colossians 1:9-11, *"For this cause we also, since the day we heard it, do not cease to pray for you, and to desire that ye might be filled with the knowledge of his will in all wisdom and spiritual understanding;* [10] *That ye might walk worthy of the Lord unto all pleasing, being fruitful in every good work, and increasing in the knowledge of God;* [11] *Strengthened with all might, according to his glorious power, unto all patience and longsuffering with joyfulness;"*

Proverbs 16:7, *"When a man's ways please the Lord, he maketh even his enemies to be at peace with him."*

PRAYER ARROWS:

- ▶ Father, I thank you for your wonderful works of creation, for creating me in your own image with a destiny, a purpose to accomplish to your glory.

- ▶ Father, I humbly ask that you give me the Spirit of wisdom and revelation so that I (YOUR NAME) your son/daughter may know You better.

Know Your Strength

- Lord, let the eyes of my understanding be enlightened in the name of Jesus.

- Father, cause my eyes to see something of the future you have called me to share, and the riches of Your glorious inheritance in the saints.

- Let me know the exceeding greatness of Your power to help me and others who believe in You.

- I thank You Lord because it is that same mighty power that raised Christ from the dead and seated Him at Your own right hand in the heavenly places.

- Lord I pray that out of Your glorious riches, you will strengthen me with power through Your Holy Spirit in my inner being in the name of Jesus.

- Let Christ dwell in my heart through faith, living within me as I trust in Him.

- Let my roots go down deep into the soil of God's marvellous love.

- Empower me to understand, with all the saints, how wide and long and high and deep the love of Christ is and to experience this love for myself.

- Father, fill me with the knowledge of Your will/purpose for my life through all spiritual wisdom and understanding in the name of Jesus.

- Let the way I live be pleasing to You always. Let me honour You so that I will always be doing good, kind things for others in the name of Jesus.

- Father, help me to grow in the knowledge of God, ever increasing and ever learning to know you better and better in Jesus' name.

- Lord, fill me with Your mighty, glorious strength so that I can keep going no matter what happens - always full of the joy of the Lord. I confess boldly and loudly: THE JOY OF THE LORD IS MY STRENGTH!

- I thank You Father, and will always thank You for making me fit to share of the wonderful things that belong to those who live in the Kingdom of Light. AMEN.

CHAPTER TWO
SWIM IN THE RIVER OF GRACE

"And He said unto me, My grace is sufficient for thee: for my strength is made perfect in weakness..." **2 Corinthians 12:9**

There is a river that must flow ceaselessly in your life if you are to take hold of all that God purposed for you. And you must swim in that river. That is the River of Grace. Do you know what **'Grace'** does? It guarantees divine settlement. In **1 Peter 5:10**, this is what the Lord says: ***"But the God of all grace, who hath called us unto his eternal glory by Christ Jesus, after that ye have suffered a while, make you perfect, stablish, strengthen, settle you."*** (emphasis added).

If you understand and pray according to this scripture, you will swim in the river of grace from now on. Let us examine the word of God in **1 Peter 5:10** carefully.

1. ***"The God of all Grace"***: The custodian, the owner of all Grace is speaking to you. Grace has many levels: great grace; abundant grace, amazing grace, sufficient grace, multiplied grace and God owns them all. Grace means unmerited favour. It is the

supernatural intervention of God in the natural affairs of men. It is Grace that makes a man to do what he cannot naturally or humanly do. WHERE RACE CANNOT TAKE YOU, GRACE WILL TAKE YOU THERE. If you are tired of running in the race of life that is producing no meaningful result, then, this is the time to cry for the Grace of God which is more than sufficient for you. **2 Corinthians 12:9**. *Grace is the Power of Christ resting upon you!*

2. *"...who hath called us unto his eternal glory by Christ Jesus"*: If you have given your life to Christ, it is the grace of God that made it possible, not your own doing. You are saved by His grace. If you are not saved or born again or you have loved ones who are not, ask the Lord to pour the oil of Grace and call them to his eternal glory by Christ Jesus. **Ephesians 2:8**. Grace brings gifts of God.

3. *"...after that ye have suffered for a while..."* Can you see the **'destiny'** of your problems? They are only **'for a while'**. Your suffering is not meant to be perpetual. **Jeremiah15:18**. Your problem has an expiry date and I declare its expiration this year in Jesus' name. Your abnormal struggles will soon be over. That is what the God of all grace has come to ensure. THE GRACE OF GOD WILL DISGRACE THEM OUT OF YOUR LIFE! By the grace of God, a way of escape has been prepared for you. Your problem is temporary; your promotion will be permanent. Your trial is temporary, your triumph is permanent. In the season of grace, the alarm clock for God to make all things beautiful for you begins to sound. This is the season. When Grace enters your door, then the time, yes, the set time to favour you has come. **Psalm 102:13**

4. 1 Peter 5:10 *"make you perfect, stablish, strengthen, settle you"*: Here comes divine perfection, establishment, strengthening and settlement. They are all the rewards of 'Grace'. When God settles you, your fishing all night without catching anything becomes past history, for you will have multitude to take home. Your years of **racing** around in life are turned to a perpetual **grazing** at the **green field of grace**. Your waiting is over, now **it is your turn**. The Bible says when the turn of Esther came (**Esther 2:15**) at the competition to choose a queen; she obtained grace that gave her the victory. (**Esther 2:17**). That is the River of Grace flowing!

To qualify to swim in the river of Grace, you must be humble, sober, yet vigilantly and forcefully resisting your adversary the devil through prayer and steadfast faith. **1 Peter 5:6-9**.

TESTIMONY: A lady testified that someone phoned her brother to confess that he had been sent to harm him and his sister (the lady). However, he had tried all manners of divination and enchantment against them with no success. He always met with a force of protection around them. This person asked if they were believers as it was only the power of Christ that could have offered them such immunity against his attacks. The point in this testimony is that while the brother and his sister were totally ignorant of the devices of the wicked against them, the 'Grace' of God was so strong upon them that the weapons fashioned against them could not prosper. You will also enjoy a similar measure of grace in the name of Jesus.

SCRIPTURES FOR MEDITATION AND PRAYER

1 Peter 5:10, *"But the God of all grace, who hath called us unto his eternal glory by Christ Jesus, after that ye have suffered a while, make you perfect, stablish, strengthen, settle you."*

2 Corinthians 12:9, *"And he said unto me, My grace is sufficient for thee: for my strength is made perfect in weakness. Most gladly therefore will I rather glory in my infirmities, that the power of Christ may rest upon me."*

Ephesians 2:8, *"For by grace are ye saved through faith; and that not of yourselves: it is the gift of God:"*

Esther 2:15-17, *"Now when the turn of Esther, the daughter of Abihail the uncle of Mordecai, who had taken her for his daughter, was come to go in unto the king, she required nothing but what Hegai the king's chamberlain, the keeper of the women, appointed. And Esther obtained favour in the sight of all them that looked upon her. [16] So Esther was taken unto king Ahasuerus into his house royal in the tenth month, which is the month Tebeth, in the seventh year of his reign. [17] And the king loved Esther above all the women, and she obtained grace and favour in his sight more than all the virgins; so that he set the royal crown upon her head, and made her queen instead of Vashti."*

Zechariah 4:7, *"Who art thou, O great mountain? before Zerubbabel thou shalt become a plain: and he shall bring forth the headstone thereof with shoutings, crying, Grace, grace unto it."*

Hebrews 4:16, *"Let us therefore come boldly unto the throne of grace, that we may obtain mercy, and find grace to help in time of need.*

PRAYER ARROWS.

▶ Lord I thank You, for by your grace I am saved and by Your grace, I will remain saved and safe in Jesus' name.

- I praise the God of all grace who has called us into his eternal glory by Christ Jesus.

- Father, you know me by name, therefore, let me find grace in your sight like never before in the name of Jesus.

- I confess and declare that this is the season of my divine perfection, divine establishment and divine settlement.

- Every problem seeking to perpetuate itself in my life, receive disgrace now by the grace of God in Jesus' name.

- This year, I quit the fruitless race of life and I enter the fruitful grace of God in the gracious name of Jesus.

- Father, terminate the season of abnormal struggles in my life and family in Jesus' mighty name.

- Lord, where race cannot take me, let Grace take me there in Jesus' name.

- Let every disgrace be converted to grace for me in the name of Jesus.

- Father, let our nation and our leaders find grace in your sight. Lead them as you led Moses and Joshua to lead Israel through the wilderness to the Promised Land in the name of Jesus.

Swim In The River Of Grace

- Father, envelope my city (name your city) in your grace and disgrace all satanic principalities out of this city in Jesus' precious name.
- Father, let me swim in your river of grace throughout this year and beyond.
- Father, as your Grace brought preference to Esther, let the same Grace give me preference in obtaining divine and natural blessings in the name of Jesus. (Name your specific desires).
- Father, let great grace be upon my church and my Pastor in the name of Jesus.
- Lord, let your grace be multiplied upon my church in our neighbourhood and let souls be added unto her daily in Jesus' name.
- By the grace of God, I will finish every good thing my hands have started and finish it well in Jesus' name.
- Every mountain before me shall crumble by the grace of God.
- Father, make all grace to abound towards me, let me always have all sufficiency in all things and let me abound to every good work in the name of Jesus.
- I confess that whatever I am going through now, the grace of God is sufficient to see me through to victory in Jesus' name.

Take It by Force! *- How To Possess Your Possessions*

- ▶ I receive the grace to be humble and remain humble in the name of Jesus.
- ▶ O Lord, grant me perpetual access to your Throne of Grace in the name of Jesus.
- ▶ Father, in my time of need, let me find grace to help in the name of Jesus.
- ▶ Thank you Father, the God of all Grace for answering my prayers.

CHAPTER THREE
I WILL NOT LET YOU GO.....

"And he said, I will not let thee go, except thou bless me" **Genesis 32:26**

One attribute of those who will **'take it by force'** is that they are persistent and persevering people in the place of prayer. They will never take 'No' for an answer. Jacob proved this attribute at the Peniel encounter in **Genesis 32**. He wrestled all night with an angel and would not let go until he took his eternal blessing. He took it by force! Jesus Christ wants us to be like that hence he told His disciples a parable in **Luke 18** to show that *"men ought always to pray and not to faint"*.

I studied Jacob's Peniel encounter and discovered sixteen ingredients of effective prayer warfare that takes it by force.

1. Prayer warfare is Worship. *"O God of my father Abraham, and God of my father Isaac..."* **Genesis 32:9**

2. Prayer warfare is standing on the promises of God and vocalising them. *"the Lord which saidst unto me, return unto thy country, and to thy kindred, and I will deal well with thee"* **Genesis 32:9**

3. Prayer warfare is humbly admitting our worthlessness before a most worthy God; confession of our depraved human state and acknowledgment of the mercies of the Most High God. *"I am not worthy of the least of all the mercies and of all the truth which thou hast shown unto thy servant..."* **Genesis 32:10**

4. Prayer warfare is approaching the throne of grace to seek mercy and help of God in time of need. **Genesis 32:10; Hebrews 4:16**

5. Prayer warfare is a cry for deliverance. Petitioning God concerning specific need, not concealing but conceding and confessing our helplessness and need for divine intervention. *"Deliver me, I pray thee, from the hand of my brother, from the hand of Esau: for I fear him, lest he will come and smite me..."* **Genesis 32:11, Psalm 34:6**

6. Prayer warfare is standing again on the word of God. *"And thou saidst. I will surely do thee good, and make thy seed as the sand of the sea..."* **Genesis 32:12**. This prayer warrior is saying based on what God has said, he and his seed cannot die or perish in the hands of Esau. You will not die in the hands of your Esau in Jesus' name. **Luke 13:33**

7. Prayer warfare is being alone with God. *"And Jacob was left alone..."* **vs.24. Mark 1:35**

8. Prayer warfare is wrestling with spiritual forces.

"and there wrestled a man with him until the breaking of the day" vs.24. Ephesians 6:12.

9. Prayer warfare is a battle of the night. *"And he rose up that night"* vs.22. Acts.16:25.

10. Prayer warfare is persistence and perseverance. It is "Operation P.U.S.H." (Pray Until Something Happens). *"I will not let thee go, except thou bless me"* vs.26.

11. Prayer warfare is travailing to prevail. *"...And the hollow of Jacob's thigh was out of joint as he wrestled with him."* vs.25. Isaiah 66:8.

12. Prayer warfare is prevailing over situation and circumstance. *"With men and hast prevailed"* vs. 28.

13. Prayer warfare must result in dominion power. *"as a prince hast thou power with God"* vs.28.

14. Prayer warfare is the avenue for transformation and change. *"Thy name shall be called no more Jacob, but Israel"* vs.28.

15. Prayer warfare is active faith: calling the things that be not as if they were already. *"My life is preserved."* vs.30. Jacob was yet to meet his hardened and vengeful brother Esau, but his fears had melted away in the place of prayer and he boldly claimed his deliverance by faith.

16. Prayer warfare is the place of divine blessing. *"And he blessed him there"* vs.29.

TESTIMONY: A revivalist, John Knox prayed earnestly to take Scotland for Christ by force. His notable prayer point was *"Lord, give me Scotland or I die"*. He prayed this prayer for many years, persistently and perseveringly. With much agonising pain and pangs, he warred against the powers of darkness. Like Jacob, he prayed until his knees left marks on the snowy sand of Scotland and he carried the mark of travail for life. But he prevailed. Heavens opened over Scotland. Even Queen Mary of Scotland had to confess: *"I fear the prayer of John Knox more than all the French armies combined"*

I challenge you to pick up a project for prayer warfare now and say *"Lord, I will not let you go until you answer me."*

SCRIPTURES FOR MEDITATION AND PRAYER

Genesis 32:9-30, *"And Jacob said, O God of my father Abraham, and God of my father Isaac, the Lord which saidst unto me, Return unto thy country, and to thy kindred, and I will deal well with thee: [10] I am not worthy of the least of all the mercies, and of all the truth, which thou hast shewed unto thy servant; for with my staff I passed over this Jordan; and now I am become two bands. [11] Deliver me, I pray thee, from the hand of my* brother, from the hand of Esau: for I fear him, lest he will come and smite me, and the mother with the children. [12] And thou saidst, I will surely do thee good, and make thy seed as the sand of the sea, which cannot be numbered for multitude. [13] And he lodged there that same night; and took of that which came to his hand a present for Esau his brother; [14] Two hundred she goats, and twenty he goats, two hundred ewes, and twenty rams, [15] Thirty milch camels with their colts, forty kine, and ten bulls, twenty she asses, and ten foals. [16] And he delivered them into the hand of his servants, every drove by themselves; and said unto his servants, Pass over before me, and put a space betwixt drove and drove. [17] And he commanded the foremost, saying, When Esau my brother meeteth thee, and asketh thee, saying, Whose art thou? and whither goest thou? and whose are these before thee? [18] Then thou shalt say, They be thy servant Jacob's; it is a present sent unto my lord Esau: and, behold, also he is behind us. [19] And so commanded he the second, and the third, and all that followed the droves, saying, On this manner shall ye speak unto Esau, when ye find him. [20] And say ye moreover, Behold, thy servant Jacob is behind us. For he said, I will appease him with the present that goeth before me, and afterward I will see his face; peradventure he will accept of me. [21] So went the present over before him: and himself lodged that night in the company. [22] And he rose up that night, and took his two wives, and his two womenservants, and his eleven sons, and passed over the ford Jabbok. [23] And he took them, and sent them over the brook, and sent over that he had. [24] And Jacob was left alone; and there wrestled a man with him until the breaking of the day. [25] And when he saw that he prevailed not against him, he touched the hollow of his thigh; and the hollow of Jacob's thigh was out of joint, as he wrestled with him. [26] And he said, Let me go, for the day breaketh. And he said, I will not let thee go, except thou bless me. [27] And he said unto him, What is thy name? And he said, Jacob. [28] And he said, Thy name shall be called no more Jacob, but Israel: for as a prince hast thou power with God and with men, and hast prevailed. [29] And Jacob asked him, and said, Tell me, I pray thee, thy name. And he said, Wherefore is it that thou dost ask after my name? And he blessed him there. [30] And Jacob called the name of the place Peniel: for I have seen God face to face, and my life is preserved."*

James 5:17-18, *"Elias was a man subject to like passions as we are, and he prayed earnestly that it might not rain: and it rained not on the earth by the space of three years and six months. [18] And he prayed again, and the heaven gave rain, and the earth brought forth her fruit."*

Esther 4:16, *"Go, gather together all the Jews that are present in Shushan, and fast ye for me, and neither eat nor drink three days, night or day: I also* and my maidens will fast likewise; and so will I go in unto the king, which is not according to the law: and if I perish, I perish."

Isaiah 38:1-5, "In those days was Hezekiah sick unto death. And Isaiah the prophet the son of Amoz came unto him, and said unto him, Thus saith the Lord, Set thine house in order: for thou shalt die, and not live. [2] Then Hezekiah turned his face toward the wall, and prayed unto the Lord, [3] And said, Remember now, O Lord, I beseech thee, how I have walked before thee in truth and with a perfect heart, and have done that which is good in thy sight. And Hezekiah wept sore. [4] Then came the word of the Lord to Isaiah, saying, [5] Go, and say to Hezekiah, Thus saith the Lord, the God of David thy father, I have heard thy prayer, I have seen thy tears: behold, I will add unto thy days fifteen years."

Mark 1:35, "And in the morning, rising up a great while before day, he went out, and departed into a solitary place, and there prayed."

Luke 18:1, "And he spake a parable unto them to this end, that men ought always to pray, and not to faint;"

Obadiah 1:17-18, "But upon mount Zion shall be deliverance, and there shall be holiness; and the house of Jacob shall possess their possessions. [18] And the house of Jacob shall be a fire, and the house *of Joseph a flame, and the house of Esau for stubble, and they shall kindle in them, and devour them; and there shall not be any remaining of the house of Esau; for the Lord hath spoken it."*

PRAYER ARROWS.

- O Lord, you are my God, I will praise you, I will exalt your name.
- I thank you Lord, for the wonderful things you are doing. Your counsel of old, they are faithful and true.
- I confess and acknowledge with gratitude your mercies over me, my family, church and city without which we would have been consumed.
- Your mercies, O God, are new every morning. Great is your faithfulness, O Lord.
- Lord, I humbly but boldly come to Your throne of grace. Lord, I obtain mercy and find grace to help in time of my need in the name of Jesus.
- Father, your word is forever settled in heaven. As your word comes down to earth through my prayers, it will not return to you void in the name of Jesus.
- O thou that hearest prayer, unto thee shall all flesh come, please answer me today by fire in the name of Jesus.

I Will Not Let You Go…..

- It is written that *"the house of Jacob shall be a fire…and the house of Esau for stubble"*. Lord, clothe me with fire and let every Esau of my life become dry grass for consumption in the name of Jesus.

- Lord, over this issue, project or matter (name the specific subject of prayer), I receive the grace to travail until I prevail in the mighty name of Jesus.

- O God, I will not let you go until you bless me in the name of Jesus.

- Lord, deliver me from the children of Esau: (Envy; Jealousy; Pride; Hatred; Vengeance and Bitterness)

- Lord, transform my life; give me a new name, a new life in Christ Jesus.

- Father, teach my hands to war and my fingers to fight in the name of Jesus.

- This year, I receive my 'Peniel' deliverance in the precious name of Jesus.

- Let every attacking Esau begin to turn back now in the name of Jesus.

- Let every hired assassins against me become voluntary bodyguards for me in the name of Jesus.

- Let all those hired to laugh at me this year begin to laugh with me in the name of Jesus.

- O Lord, let no one have any cause to say 'sorry' to me all the days of my life in the merciful name of Jesus.
- In the name of Jesus, I shall reach my Canaan, I shall possess my possessions.
- You powers contending with my well of inheritance, scatter by fire in the name of Jesus.
- Let the Sun of Glory and Righteousness rise upon me in the mighty name of Jesus.
- You Esau, you will not kill my star, I shall arise and shine in the name of Jesus.
- Lord, make it impossible for the people of my city to go to hell in the name of Jesus.
- I receive the grace for ceaseless intercession for my city in the saving name of Jesus.
- As *"Esau returned that day on his way unto Seir"* so will all my enemies turn back in the powerful name of Jesus Christ.
- Thank you Father, this year, I will celebrate the victory you have given me in every area of my life in Jesus' name.

CHAPTER FOUR
I SHALL GO VERY FAR

"And Pharaoh said, I will let you go, that ye may sacrifice to the Lord your God in the wilderness; only ye shall not go very far away..." **Exodus 8:28**

God's plan for you is to be totally free from enemy domination and manipulation. But your freedom is not cheap. Jesus Christ paid with His blood. You must also fight to ascertain and maintain your freedom.

In **Exodus 8:1**, the Lord spoke to Moses that he should go and tell Pharaoh **"Thus saith the Lord, let my people go that they may serve me"** That was God's kingdom agenda for freedom. Even then, God knew that the freedom will have to be won by force, for we read in **Exodus 10:20** that the Lord hardened Pharaoh's heart so that he will not let the children of Israel go. The Lord who hardened the heart of your oppressor will also melt it in Jesus' name.

Four major tactics of the enemy are revealed in the way Pharaoh responded to Moses' demand for freedom:

1. In **Exodus 5:1-2**, Pharaoh told Moses that he does not know the Lord and so he will not let Israel go.

We learn from this that the enemy does not want his victim to be free at all. He wants to perpetuate the affliction or the enslavement of his victim. **Luke 13:16; Mark 11:1-10.** This is the reason why some die unsaved, die poor; die undelivered from affliction. This is the spirit behind people who give up, commit suicide or simply resign themselves to fate.

2. In **Exodus 8:25-28**, Pharaoh again responded to the demand for freedom by saying to Moses: Alright your people can go and sacrifice to their God but *"only you shall not go very far away"*. We learn here that the enemy can concede **temporary freedom** but not a permanent one. He can say, be free for a while, but then I have the right to always come back to you. He wants to maintain a territorial foothold over your destiny. He says: Don't ever be on fire for God. Be lukewarm: hot today, and cold tomorrow. Those who backslide suffer from this syndrome. This is also the spirit behind recurring problems and the fear of them. Many repeated tragedies or recurring problems are due to this. Note that when Jesus cast out the legion of demons from the madman of Gadarene, those demons did not want to go very far away. (See **Mark 5:10**). They wanted to be close enough to their victim so that they can stage a comeback as soon as possible. I decree today that affliction will not rise up a second time in your life in Jesus' name. The enemy says you must not go very far (spiritually, physically, materially etc).Will you agree?

3. Another one of the tactics of the enemy is revealed in **Exodus10:7-9**. Pharaoh told Moses: Now, I will let you go, but only the men, leave all the women and children behind. The enemy can concede to **partial freedom** but not total. Partial freedom is when he says you can be free in some areas of your life, but let him have control of some other areas. He may let you go, but then hold unto your children. This is the cause of many generational problems. The enemy wants to perpetuate enslavement across generations. The enemy can allow a father to be great for God but the children grow rebellious like Eli and his children. He can concede wealth to some but take hold of their health contrary to the word and will of God. **3 John 2**.

4. In **Exodus 10:24**, Pharaoh pulled another joker by saying to Moses, *"Go serve the Lord, only let your flocks and your herds be stayed..."* This is what I call 'QUALIFIED OR CONDITIONAL FREEDOM'. The enemy says 'Okay, go, worship the Lord with all your heart, your body and your mind but not with your substance. Let me control that'. So every time you say, I love God so much and you show it in every way, but when it comes to giving of tithes and offering, you hesitate, that is the enemy tactics at work in your life. This is the prince controlling the children of disobedience and partial obedience.

The remedy for all the wiles of the enemy is to resist him fiercely as Moses' did. **1 Peter 5:9**, *"Whom resist stedfast in the faith, knowing that the same afflictions are accomplished in your brethren that are in the world."*

On each occasion, Moses rejected Pharaoh's demonic suggestion. He insisted on TAKING IT ALL and by force if need be. Moses succeeded; you too will succeed in Jesus' name. Learn and apply the following six principles and you will go very far in the name of Jesus.

1. Know that it is God's will for you to BE TOTALLY FREE. **John 8:36**; **Exodus 3:7-8**. So make up your mind that you will not negotiate your INDEED FREEDOM from enemy control, domination and manipulation. **Exodus 10:25-26; Nehemiah 4:10-12**

2. You must refuse the devil's advocate's alternatives. It looks like freedom, but it is not really freedom. Be careful and be discerning in your choices.

3. You must have an answer for every fiery arrow the enemy throws at you and your answer must be based on the word of God. **Ephesians 6:17**.

4. Keep praying all manners of prayers until God's ultimate judgment descends upon your unrepentant Pharaoh. **Exodus11:1; Exodus 12:37**

5. Do not be afraid.

6. Do not be discouraged.

7. Live a life of uncompromising holiness that keeps you far away from the enemy and vice versa.

TESTIMONY: A lady was given a four-year work permit and leave to remain in the country for the same period. However, she believed strongly that she was entitled to an indefinite leave to remain and unlimited permit to work. She pondered over the issue and made up her mind to pursue it with the Home Office. She sought counsel from some close friends and colleagues and they all advised her not to pursue the matter. She ought to be satisfied with the four-year visa she has been given. (Temporary, partial freedom). She prayed and fasted over the matter and her conviction did not change. Early one morning, she went to the Home Office, did some prophetic warfare and boldly confronted the officials. Her claim sounded ridiculously to them initially but at last, she left the Home Office that same day with an Indefinite Leave to Remain and work in the country.

When you make up your mind that you will go very far, the irreversible shall be reversed in Jesus' name.

SCRIPTURES FOR MEDITATION AND PRAYER

Exodus 3:7-9, *"And the Lord said, I have surely seen the affliction of my people which are in Egypt, and have heard their cry by reason of their taskmasters; for I know their sorrows; [8] And I am come down to deliver them out of the hand of the Egyptians, and to bring them up out of that land unto a good land and a large, unto a land flowing with milk and honey; unto the place of the Canaanites, and the Hittites, and the Amorites, and the Perizzites, and the Hivites, and the Jebusites. [9] Now therefore, behold, the cry of the children of Israel is come unto me: and I have also seen the oppression wherewith the Egyptians oppress them."*

Exodus 5:1-2, *"And afterward Moses and Aaron went in, and told Pharaoh, Thus saith the Lord God of Israel, Let my people go, that they may hold a feast unto me in the wilderness. [2] And Pharaoh said, Who is the Lord, that I should obey his voice to let Israel go? I know not the Lord, neither will I let Israel go."*

Exodus 8:25-28, *"And Pharaoh called for Moses and for Aaron, and said, Go ye, sacrifice to your God in the land. [26] And Moses said, It is not meet so to do; for we shall sacrifice the abomination of the Egyptians to the Lord our God: lo, shall we sacrifice the abomination of the Egyptians before their eyes, and will they not stone us?* [27] *We will go three days' journey into the wilderness, and sacrifice to the Lord our God, as he shall command us.* [28] *And Pharaoh said, I will let you go, that ye may sacrifice to the Lord your God in the wilderness; only ye shall not go very far away: intreat for me."*

Exodus 10:7-9, *"And Pharaoh's servants said unto him, How long shall this man be a snare unto us? let the men go, that they may serve the Lord their God: knowest thou not yet that Egypt is destroyed?* [8] *And Moses and Aaron were brought again unto Pharaoh: and he said unto them, Go, serve the Lord your God: but who are they that shall go?* [9] *And Moses said, We will go with our young and with our old, with our sons and with our daughters, with our flocks and with our herds will we go; for we must hold a feast unto the Lord."*

Exodus 10:24, *"And Pharaoh called unto Moses, and said, Go ye, serve the Lord; only let your flocks and your herds be stayed: let your little ones also go with you."*

Exodus 11:1, *"And the Lord said unto Moses, Yet will I bring one plague more upon Pharaoh, and upon Egypt; afterwards he will let you go hence: when he shall let you go, he shall surely thrust you out hence altogether."*

Luke 13:16, *"And ought not this woman, being a*

daughter of Abraham, whom Satan hath bound, lo, these eighteen years, be loosed from this bond on the sabbath day?"

Mark 11:1-2, *"And when they came nigh to Jerusalem, unto Bethphage and Bethany, at the mount of Olives, he sendeth forth two of his disciples, [2] And saith unto them, Go your way into the village over against you: and as soon as ye be entered into it, ye shall find a colt tied, whereon never man sat; loose him, and bring him."*

John 8:36, *"If the Son therefore shall make you free, ye shall be free indeed."*

Nehemiah 4:10-12, *"And Judah said, The strength of the bearers of burdens is decayed, and there is much rubbish; so that we are not able to build the wall. [11] And our adversaries said, They shall not know, neither see, till we come in the midst among them, and slay them, and cause the work to cease. [12] And it came to pass, that when the Jews which dwelt by them came, they said unto us ten times, From all places whence ye shall return unto us they will be upon you."*

Ephesians 6:17-18, *"And take the helmet of salvation, and the sword of the Spirit, which is the word of God: [18] Praying always with all prayer and supplication in the Spirit, and watching thereunto with all perseverance and supplication for all saints;"*

PRAYER ARROWS

- Lord I thank you for the saving grace of our Lord Jesus Christ which gave me total freedom from all the powers of darkness.

- Lord, open my eyes to recognise the tricks and the tactics of the enemy in my life, in my family, church and city in the name of Jesus.

- Lord, send one more plague to every Pharaoh that will not let the souls in this city go and serve their Maker.

- I command the land, the air and the waters to withdraw their co-operation with all the powers of darkness operating in this nation in the name of Jesus.

- Pharaoh, the Lord of the Hebrews has met with me, I announce the end of your enslavement over me and my family in Jesus' name.

- Let every problem see the finger of God.

- I declare that I will go very far! Every Pharaoh that will not let me go far, become a guest at the bed of the Red Sea in the name of Jesus.

- O you Pharaoh of my life, I declare that you are a mere noise, your time has expired. Pack your load and get out of my life in the name of Jesus.

- Let every troubler of my Israel receive permanent

- assignment of confusion and scattering of tongues in Jesus' name.
- I refuse temporary, partial or conditional freedom. I demand total freedom from oppression, depression and regression in the name of Jesus.
- Holy Spirit, reveal to me every tactic and strategy of the enemy.
- Let every device of the wicked be disappointed so that they are not able to perform their enterprise in the mighty name of Jesus.
- In the name of Jesus, I possess my salvation and deliverance from the claws of Pharaoh.
- In the name of Jesus, I possess my spouse, children, relations and loved ones from the jaws of Pharaoh.
- In the name of Jesus, I possess my peace, joy, gentleness, patience from the snare of Pharaoh.
- In the name of Jesus, I possess my health and wealth from the attack of Pharaoh.
- Every Pharaoh that will not allow my church enjoy the freedom of worship will have problem at the red sea in the name of Jesus.
- In the name of Jesus, I will not leave this day, this week, this month, this year empty handed. I shall be a candidate for favour!

I Shall Go Very Far

- Let all those who stood to oppose me bombard me with congratulatory messages this year in the mighty name of Jesus.

- I declare that the people of my city will go up to worship the Lord and the gate of Pharaoh will not prevail in the name of Jesus Christ.

- I reject every manipulation and temptations of Pharaoh. By the grace of God, I shall live in obedience to the words of my God in Jesus' name.

- I reject the spirit of fear. I paralyse your operations; I cast you out of my life.

- Let every foothold of the enemy in my life be removed.

- This year, I will go forward. Pharaoh will not slow me down in the name of Jesus.

- I confess, I have a goal to reach, I am Canaan bound, and my life will not waste in Jesus' precious name.

- O Lord, the journey before me is long, satisfy my hunger with the Bread of Heaven; quench my thirst with the living water in the name of Jesus.

- Thank you Father, for rescuing my destiny from the ferocity of Pharaoh.

CHAPTER FIVE

MY HAIR WILL GROW AGAIN!

"Howbeit the hair of his head began to grow again…" **Judges 16:22**

Samson was a child of destiny. He was a miracle child, conceived after an angel came to announce the end of barrenness in the lives of his parents. **Judges 13:2-5** Today, I announce that barrenness has come to an end in your life in the name of Jesus.

As a special child, there were specific instructions to be observed in bringing him up and in his lifestyle. The mother shall neither drink wine nor eat any unclean thing. The child's hair must never be cut for he shall be a Nazarene, anointed servant of God from the womb who will begin to deliver Israel from the Philistines.

Jesus paid a price with his blood to redeem us. Once we are born again, we become special children. We cannot do as we please. There are specific commands we must observe in order to be all He wants us to become. **2 Corinthians 5:17; Exodus 15:26**. This is why we are called a peculiar people. **1 Peter 2:9**. We are also called a peculiar treasure. **Exodus 19:5**. The devil too is aware of who you are so he looses all his agents to go all out to make sure you disobey God and lose your status in Christ.

That is what they did to Samson. They laid a snare or siege around him until he fell into it and his hair of destiny was shaved off. You will not fall into the snare of the fowler in Jesus' name.

The *'hair'* represents the strength, power, virtue, grace, purpose, destiny, gift and the anointing of God in the life of a person. When the hair of a person is at the risk of being vandalized by the enemy, you will notice some traits like the following:

1. A man whose hair is under attack would begin to go the wrong direction, make wrong choices of company, location and pastime. In **Judges 16:1**, the Bible says that Samson went to Gaza and began an affair with a harlot. One translation says *"there he saw a loose woman"* (BIBE). When a man yields his manhood to a loose woman, he begins to lose and can never gain from the enterprise.

2. A person whose hair is about to go under the satanic barber's razor will begin to operate at below capacity level. **Judges 16:3**. What on earth was Samson doing with the load on his shoulders. This was not the Samson we knew in **Judges 15:12-15**. He didn't kill the enemies, he was carrying their luggage. **Pray aloud:** *I will not carry the load of the enemy in Jesus' name. Let every evil load be consumed by fire in the name of Jesus.*

3. They become weak, spiritually and physically. Prayer time drops, sensitivity to the Holy Spirit drops. They no longer hear from God. **1 Samuel 28:6.** They become like a dog that no longer hears the whistle of the hunter. The spirit of error takes over. **Judges 16:4.** Samson has now graduated from the harlot of Gaza to Delilah of the Valley of Sorek (*'Sorek'* means hissing). Valley means pit. This man is sinking into the valley where the enemies will hiss at him. Delilah means poor, small. Samson the great is now fellowshipping with Delilah the small, the poor! Of what fellowship has light got with darkness? Pray aloud: I shall never become an object of hissing. I will not be joined to poverty. I dissolve every association with mean men in Jesus' name.

4. They acquire a slumbering and sleeping spirit giving the enemy good grounds to attack. They can sleep so deep until witches and wizards have eaten them up for supper. **Matthew 13:25; Judges 16:19; 1 Samuel 26:12.** No more night vigils. They suffer regular defeats, repeated tragedies and recurring afflictions. Delilah used demonic tranquilizer to send Samson to a deep sleep of death. Samson has backslidden! He used to be a midnight Christian (See **Judges 16:3** 'rising at midnight') Now, he is a sleeping Christian. You will not sleep the sleep of death in Jesus' name.

5. They lose control of their sexual appetite. They fornicate and commit adultery with reckless abandon. The moment king Solomon began to love many strange women, the hair of his destiny was at risk. **1 Kings 11:1**. In **Judges 16:16**, Delilah pressed Samson daily until his soul was *'vexed unto death'*. His body was already under witchcraft control, now his soul has been subdued. Very soon, he will lose his spirit. May the fire of God consume every power vexing your soul in the name of Jesus.

6. They become power-driven instead of spirit-driven. Profitless hard labour replaces profitable high favour. In **Judges 16:20**, Samson thought he still had the anointing. It is very dangerous for a man to still think he has the anointing when the Lord had long left him. When a minister stands on a pulpit that has no God's presence, it is no more a pulpit, but a pull-pit, ready to pull him down into the pit! It is not by might nor by power, but by the Spirit of God. **Zechariah 4:6**.

7. They lose vision, direction or focus. Samson's eyes were plucked out as soon as his hair was shaved. **Judges 16:21**; **Proverbs 29:18**, *"Where there is no vision, the people perish: but he that keepeth the law, happy is he."*

RESTORATION IS POSSIBLE.

Judges.16:22, *"Howbeit, the hair of his head began to grow again..."*. Samson's strength was restored when his hair began to grow again. It is possible that you were doing well before but it's no longer so, your hair will grow again. May be you used to enjoy good health but it's no longer so, your hair will grow again. It could be that some organs have failed to perform or grown weary in your body. In as much as the hair is an organ of the body and it can grow again, I prophesy that the Holy Ghost will jump start those organs NOW!

WHAT WILL MAKE YOUR HAIR GROW AGAIN?

1. You must not write yourself off. You may be a backslider, but know that God is a God of second chance. You can front slide again. The prodigal son did not write himself off. Don't resign to fate.

2. Repent from your transgression. David sinned but he repented and his hair grew again. A sincere and genuine prayer of repentance will not go unnoticed by God. **Psalm 51:1-17.**

3. Cry to God in prayer for divine remembrance like Samson. **Judges 16:28.**

4. Expect help to come your way from unexpected quarters. **Judges 16:26; 1 Samuel 30:11**

5. Do not focus on your disability, focus on God's ability. Disability is not a barrier; it is a bonus when surrendered to Jesus.

6. Samson's physical eyes were plucked out, but his spiritual eyes of understanding were kept opened. Keep your faith and your dream alive.

TESTIMONIES

ONE: Peter Daniels suffered dyslexia, inability to read and was still an illiterate at the age of 26. However, he surrendered his life to Christ and called upon God at a Billy Graham crusade. Few years later, he had read 2000 books, trained himself in Law, Business, Philosophy and became one of the best public speakers in the world, most successful businessman in Australia and one of the greatest Philanthropists alive today. His hair of destiny grew again!

TWO: Fanny Jane Crosby became eye-infected at the age of six weeks. Five years later, doctors told her she would never see again. Her grandmother began to read the Bible to her. She developed her memory and soon, she had memorised almost the entire Bible. In her lifetime, she composed more than 6000 hymns. Great hymns such as ***Pass Me not O Gentle Saviour, To God Be the Glory, I am Thine O Lord, Blessed Assurance*** were composed by her. She died at age 95 in fame and not in shame. On her tomb at Connecticut is inscribed the words *"Blessed Assurance, Jesus is Mine. Oh What a foretaste of Glory divine"*. Her hair of destiny grew again!

THREE: Following a prayer meeting I was privileged to lead in Italy a few years ago, a woman came to testify the following day. She slept after the meeting and in a dream; she heard a voice telling her to look ahead of her. She saw a tall giant looking fellow in shining white garment. The voice said to her "That is the ANGEL I have sent to roll away your reproach". She woke up from her dream, struck with fear and relief at the same time. She felt like going to the toilet. On getting there, she started menstruating for the first time after about ten years of cessation. Her hair of destiny began to grow again! This will be your testimony this year in Jesus' name.

They only shaved your hair from the outside, the root is in the inside, and it can grow again. *"For there is hope of a tree, if it be cut down, that it will sprout again, and that the tender branch thereof will not cease".* **Job 14:7**

Samson killed more enemies when he had no eyes than when he had eyes. God can turn any disability to ability.

My Hair Will Grow Again!

SCRIPTURES FOR MEDITATION AND PRAYER

Judges 16:4-5,15-22, *"And it came to pass afterward, that he loved a woman in the valley of Sorek, whose name was Delilah. [5] And the lords of the Philistines came up unto her, and said unto her, Entice him, and see wherein his great strength lieth, and by what means we may prevail against him, that we may bind him to afflict him: and we will give thee every one of us eleven hundred pieces of silver. [15] And she said unto him, How canst thou say, I love thee, when thine heart is not with me? thou hast mocked me these three times, and hast not told me wherein thy great strength lieth. [16] And it came to pass, when she pressed him daily with her words, and urged him, so that his soul was vexed unto death; [17] That he told her all his heart, and said unto her, There hath not come a razor upon mine head; for I have been a Nazarite unto God from my mother's womb: if I be shaven, then my strength will go from me, and I shall become weak, and be like any other man. [18] And when Delilah saw that he had told her all his heart, she sent and called for the lords of the Philistines, saying, Come up this once, for he hath shewed me all his heart. Then the lords of the Philistines came up unto her, and brought money in their hand. [19] And she made him sleep upon her knees; and she called for a man, and she caused him* to shave off the seven locks of his head; and she began to afflict him, and his strength went from him. [20] *And she said, The Philistines be upon thee, Samson. And he awoke out of his sleep, and said, I will go out as at other times before, and shake myself. And he wist not that the Lord was departed from him.* [21] *But the Philistines took him, and put out his eyes, and brought him down to Gaza, and bound him with fetters of brass; and he did grind in the prison house.* [22] *Howbeit the hair of his head began to grow again after he was shaven."*

Matthew 13:25, *"But while men slept, his enemy came and sowed tares among the wheat, and went his way."*

Job 14:7, *"For there is hope of a tree, if it be cut down, that it will sprout again, and that the tender branch thereof will not cease."*

Job 42:10-17, *"And the Lord turned the captivity of Job, when he prayed for his friends: also the Lord gave Job twice as much as he had before.* [11] *Then came there unto him all his brethren, and all his sisters, and all they that had been of his acquaintance before, and did eat bread with him in his house: and they bemoaned him, and comforted him over all the evil that the Lord had brought upon him: every man also gave him a piece of money, and every one an earring of gold.* [12] *So the Lord blessed the latter end of Job more than his beginning: for he* had fourteen thousand sheep, and six thousand camels, and a thousand yoke of oxen, and a thousand she asses. [13] He had also seven sons and three daughters. [14] And he called the name of the first, Jemima; and the name of the second, Kezia; and the name of the third, Keren-happuch. [15] And in all the land were no women found so fair as the daughters of Job: and their father gave them inheritance among their brethren. [16] After this lived Job an hundred and forty years, and saw his sons, and his sons' sons, even four generations. [17] So Job died, being old and full of days."

1 Kings 11:1, "But king Solomon loved many strange women, together with the daughter of Pharaoh, women of the Moabites, Ammonites, Edomites, Zidonians, and Hittites;"

Psalm 51:10-13, "Create in me a clean heart, O God; and renew a right spirit within me. [11] Cast me not away from thy presence; and take not thy holy spirit from me. [12] Restore unto me the joy of thy salvation; and uphold me with thy free spirit. [13] Then will I teach transgressors thy ways; and sinners shall be converted unto thee."

PRAYER ARROWS:

▶ Father, forgive me for every sin that has landed me into trouble in the name of Jesus. Have mercy on me O Lord.

- I refuse to cooperate with the enemy to destroy my destiny in Jesus' name.
- Every Delilah operating in my life, die by fire.
- Lord, do not hand me over to the will of my enemy in the name of Jesus.
- Let every reward of divination issued out for my sake catch fire in the name of Jesus.
- I command every gang up to afflict me to scatter by fire in the name of Jesus Christ.
- I recover every ground that I have lost to the enemy in the name of Jesus.
- Lord, remember me, let my hair grow again in the name of Jesus.
- Lord, protect me in my unguarded hour in the name of Jesus.
- Let every satanic web of enticement and entrapment catch fire now in Jesus' mighty name.
- In the name of Jesus, my soul will never become a captive of the satanic net of the fowler.
- Let all the web of sickness, untimely death, failure, poverty and stagnation be consumed by fire in Jesus' powerful name.
- I declare loud and clear that the snare of Delilah over my life is permanently and forever broken in the name of Jesus Christ.

- Let every house of Delilah built for my sake be pulled down and become dilapidated in Jesus' mighty name.
- By the anointing that destroys the yoke, I denounce Delilah's influence; I destroy Delilah's throne; I demolish Delilah's altar out of my life in the name of Jesus.
- I will not sleep the sleep of death in the name of Jesus.
- I will not be a victim of Delilah's tranquilizer in the name of Jesus.
- Led every poison of spiritual slumbering and backsliding injected into me be neutralized by the powerful blood of Jesus.
- Lord let the fire of your glory keep burning afresh upon the altar of our church. Let it never go out in the name of Jesus.
- O Lord, rekindle the fire of prayer in my life and let every ashes of prayerlessness disappear in the name of Jesus.
- Father, save my head from satanic barbers in the name of Jesus.
- Father, save my hair from the hand of destiny destroyers in the mighty name of Jesus.
- You spirits of lust, immorality and pride, be far away from me in the precious name of Jesus.

- I receive the grace to keep my body under subjection and self discipline in the name of Jesus.
- Father, deliver me from these three potential destroyers: POWER, MONEY and SEX.
- Let the lap of every Delilah sent against Ministers of God catch fire now in the name of Jesus.
- Every Delilah, operating in the church, be exposed and expelled by fire in the name of Jesus.
- Daughters of Delilah, die by fire in the name of Jesus.
- Every satanic razor aimed at my hair of glory; catch fire now in the name of Jesus.
- I shall not end up in the valley of Sorek (hissing). I will not become a laughing stock or object of hissing to the enemies of my star in Jesus' name.
- Holy Ghost, jump-start every organ of my body that is not functioning or functioning below capacity in the name of Jesus.
- Father, reactivate the tender branch of my destiny; let it not cease in the name of Jesus.
- Every barber hired from the pit of hell to destroy me, die by fire in the name of Jesus.
- Father, let every good tree the enemy had cut off in my life sprout again to your glory.

My Hair Will Grow Again!

- O Lord, cast me not away from your presence, take not your Holy spirit from me, restore unto me the joy of my salvation and renew the right spirit within me in the name of Jesus.

- Every fallen saint shall rise again in the name of Jesus Christ. Every backslidden Christian shall front slide again in Jesus' name.

- Thank you Father, for restoring my hair of joy, peace, salvation, destiny and fulfilment.

CHAPTER SIX

I WILL RECOVER ALL! (OPERATION ZIGLAG)

"Pursue: for thou shalt surely overtake them, and without fail recover all." **1 Samuel 30:8**

To recover all means to regain completely what was taken away from you. God's desire for us is to have a balanced life and all round well being. *"He hath done all things well"* **Mark 7:37**. In **Genesis 1:31,** *"God saw everything that he had made and behold it was very good."* That includes you. In fact, you were the best of all he made. Whatever is less than very good in your life is not your original state and you must fight to recover your total being.

In **3 John 2**, we have proof of God's desire for a three dimensional prosperity for you: *"Beloved, I wish above all things that thou mayest prosper and be in health, even as thy soul prospereth"* Here we can see Spiritual prosperity; Material prosperity and Physical prosperity. Whichever is missing now in your life was stolen by the enemy and you must take it back by force. The enemy launched an SKD (Steal, Kill and Destroy) attack against you (Jn.10:10). You must launch a GKP (Goliath Killing Prayers) counterattack to take it all back. You can be an all round success. David proved it. He was a successful soldier but the devil wanted him to fail as a successful husband. He fought and recovered his lost family. You can replace some things that are stolen for example, television set or car, but you cannot replace others; you must recover them like your health, your wife, and your children.

STRATEGIES FOR TAKING IT ALL BACK:

1. TAKE RESPONSIBILITY: Who are you blaming for your woes? Many marriages will be saved if the couple stops passing the buck. What you need is action, not reaction. Do not be a reactionary. David did not blame anyone. All blamed him but he blamed none. You should do the same.

- GARY COLEMAN: The highest paid child star in the 80s earning $64,000 a week. He became bankrupt in 1995. Who is at fault? He said: "I can spread the blame all the way around, from me, to my accountants, to my adoptive parents, to agents, to lawyers and back to me again."

2. DON'T KEEP COMPANY WITH WAILERS AND WEEPERS. 1 Samuel 30:4, *"Then David and the people that were with him lifted up their voice and wept, until they had no more power to weep."*

Mourning, murmuring, complaining, grumbling,

lamenting will not solve any problem. Jesus Christ always got rid of weepers and wailers before he could perform miracles. **Mark.5:40**. You must do the same. Get angry at the robber of your destiny not at yourself. Don't throw a pity-party. Get rid of sympathetic undertakers. Tell them it's not your funeral time yet! **Philippians 4:6-8**. Anxiety, fear and worry will not solve any problem, they'll add more. Don't allow your weeping to endure beyond the night. **Psalm 30:5**.

3. ENCOURAGE YOURSELF IN THE LORD. 1 Samuel 30:6, *"And David was greatly distressed; for the people spake of stoning him, because the soul of all the people was grieved, every man for his sons and for his daughters: but David encouraged himself in the Lord his God."*

Courage, success and victory do not come through people encouraging you, it comes through you encouraging yourself in the Lord. **Joshua 1:8**. The way to **turn pressure to pleasure** is to encourage yourself in the Lord. **Defeat does not have to breed depression** in your life. **Failure is not final. Delay is not denial. Setback is not a bar to a comeback.** In **Judges 20:22**, Israel was defeated in battle, yet they encouraged themselves in the Lord. By the next day, their defeat had turned to victory.

4. **ENQUIRE FROM THE LORD.** **1 Samuel 30:7-8,** *"And David said to Abiathar the priest, Ahimelech's son, I pray thee, bring me hither the ephod. And Abiathar brought thither the ephod to David. [8] And David enquired at the Lord, saying, Shall I pursue after this troop? shall I overtake them? And he answered him, Pursue: for thou shalt surely overtake them, and without fail recover all."*

If you want to recover all, you must check things out with God. The fact that you are desperate to succeed is no licence to violate God's will and purpose. **Jeremiah 33:3.** Many are pursuing in the wrong direction because they did not inquire from God and so it's not God leading them. They are flesh-led not spirit-led. The way to enquire from the Lord is to dig deep into His word concerning your situation; find out what He says; pray continually; wait on Him until you pray through and receive the peace of God concerning specific steps to take.

5. **YOU MUST PURSUE.** *"But David pursued, he and four hundred men..."* **1 Samuel 30:10.** God had long given many the green light, yet they are still sitting down, praying, hearing from the Lord. Faith without works is dead. What you pursue, you recover and what you recover you possess. In **Genesis 25:22-26,** Jacob fought all the way; he kept pursuing and recovered his blessings from Esau.

6. **OVERTAKE.** *"Pursue, for thou shall surely overtake them and without fail recover all."* **1 Samuel 30:8.** To overtake is to catch up with or surpass. It means to go over and take. The enemy is on the run with your destiny. It must be a hot chase. This is the place of persistent, persevering prayers. You don't give up until you take up. No retreat, no surrender. David said he leapt over the wall, ran through the troops and broke the bow of steel. **2 Samuel 22:30,35.** Note that God did not say he will go and get what was stolen for David. He will only back him up. The Holy Spirit is your back up in prayer; He is not your substitute. **Romans 8:26.**

7. **HELP THOSE YOU MEET ON THE WAY.** 1 Samuel 30:11-15, *"And they found an Egyptian in the field, and brought him to David, and gave him bread, and he did eat; and they made him drink water; [12] And they gave him a piece of a cake of figs, and two clusters of raisins: and when he had eaten, his spirit came again to him: for he had eaten no bread, nor drunk any water, three days and three nights. [13] And David said unto him, To whom belongest thou? and whence art thou? And he said, I am a young man of Egypt, servant to an Amalekite; and my master left me, because three days agone I fell sick. [14] We made an invasion upon the south of the Cherethites, and upon the coast which belongeth to Judah, and upon the south of Caleb; and we burned Ziklag with fire. [15] And David said*

to him, Canst thou bring me down to this company? And he said, Swear unto me by God, that thou wilt neither kill me, nor deliver me into the hands of my master, and I will bring thee down to this company."

The way up is down. As you go up in pursuit, look down occasionally and help those who are fallen. They may hold the key to your breakthrough. As Joseph interpreted the dream of common criminals, little did he know that one of them held the key to his own dream? **Genesis 40. The best way to remain blessed is to keep on being a blessing. The dead sea is dead because it gives nothing out but collects everything. When you help others to recover, you are on your way to recovery too.** Remember the law of sowing and reaping. Practice the law of completion and avoid the rule of competition.

8. EXPECT UNUSUAL HELPERS OF DESTINY. 1 Samuel 30:11-16. The man that helped David's company was in the camp of the enemies that raided his town of Ziklag. The men who came to help David secure the crown in **1 Chronicles 12** were once **debtors, discontented** and **distressed** folks. **1 Samuel 22**. A slave girl gave Naaman the clue that led to his recovery. **1 Kings 5**. A woman killed General Sisera who oppressed Israel for 20 years. **Judges 4:21**. A young boy exposed the secret plot to kill Paul. **Acts 23:16**. May God raise help for you from unexpected quarters this year in Jesus' name. **Isaiah 60:10.** Pray aloud: *Father, raise help for me from unusual quarters.*

9. RECOVER ALL. 1 Samuel 30:18-19, *"And David recovered all that the Amalekites had carried away: and David rescued his two wives. [19] And there was nothing lacking to them, neither small nor great, neither sons nor daughters, neither spoil, nor any thing that they had taken to them: David recovered all."*

Do not leave the enemy half dead. Cut off the head of Goliath as well. Do all things well. Take it all back. Don't just fast to be healed, fast and pray to be made whole. Use all the weapons of warfare at your disposal. Break through to Your breakthroughs. See that child return to the Lord. See that husband return home. See your wife pregnant; see that job in your hands. See that application succeed. Whatever you have given up on, pursue, overtake and take it up in total recovery. You ought always to pray and not to faint. Keep travailing until you prevail. Your labour pain will soon result in favour-birth! **There will be no abandoned project in your life this year in the name of Jesus.**

10. GIVE GOD THE GLORY. 1 Samuel 30:22-23, *"Then answered all the wicked men and men of Belial, of those that went with David, and said, Because they went not with us, we will not give them* *ought of the spoil that we have recovered, save to every man his wife and his children, that they may lead them away, and depart.* [23] *Then said David, Ye shall not do so, my brethren, with that which the Lord hath given us, who hath preserved us, and delivered the company that came against us into our hand."*

Jesus is your ultimate Recoverer. Don't ever push Him aside or share the glory with Him. Dedicate your victories to Him forever and He shall make it permanent. You are to possess your possessions, never allow your possessions possess you. The best way to defeat greed and selfishness in life is to acknowledge God as the source of all things and the giver of all things. We brought nothing to this world and nothing we will take with us. Your first step towards total recovery now is to acknowledge Jesus as your Lord and Saviour and surrender to Him completely. Keep thanking and praising Him for victory.

TESTIMONY: A lady testified that when her father died, her mother and the children were thrown into abject poverty as a result of her father's relations' decision to sit on their inheritance. They were wrongly disinherited and forced to live in undeserved penury. There seemed to be no hope anywhere including the court of law. She and her siblings took the matter to the Court of God. They battled in prayers for years to recover all that the adversaries had stolen. Recently, Heaven responded, her deceased father's relations called her Mother, apologised for their wrongdoings and began to surrender all that they had taken. A journey to total recovery started for this family. Praise God! **I decree that everything the enemy had stolen from you shall be returned sevenfold in the name of Jesus.**

SCRIPTURES FOR MEDITATION AND PRAYER

1 Samuel 30:1-8, *"And it came to pass, when David and his men were come to Ziklag on the third day, that the Amalekites had invaded the south, and Ziklag, and smitten Ziklag, and burned it with fire;* **[2]** *And had taken the women captives, that were therein: they slew not any, either great or small, but carried them away, and went on their way.* **[3]** *So David and his men came to the city, and, behold, it was burned with fire; and their wives, and their sons, and their daughters, were taken captives.* **[4]** *Then David and the people that were with him lifted up their voice and wept, until they had no more power to weep.* **[5]** *And David's two wives were taken captives, Ahinoam the Jezreelitess, and Abigail the wife of Nabal the Carmelite.* **[6]** *And David was greatly distressed; for the people spake of stoning him, because the soul of all the people was grieved, every man for his sons and for his daughters: but*

I Will Recover All! (Operation Ziglag)

David encouraged himself in the Lord his God. [7] *And David said to Abiathar the priest, Ahimelech's son, I pray thee, bring me hither the ephod. And Abiathar brought thither the ephod to David.* [8] *And David enquired at the Lord, saying, Shall I pursue after this troop? shall I overtake them? And he answered him, Pursue: for thou shalt surely overtake them, and without fail recover all."*

John 10:10, *"The thief cometh not, but for to steal, and to kill, and to destroy: I am come that they might have life, and that they might have it more abundantly."*

3 John 1:2, *"Beloved, I wish above all things that thou mayest prosper and be in health, even as thy soul prospereth."*

Judges 4:21-22, *"Then Jael Heber's wife took a nail of the tent, and took an hammer in her hand, and went softly unto him, and smote the nail into his temples, and fastened it into the ground: for he was fast asleep and weary. So he died.* [22] *And, behold, as Barak pursued Sisera, Jael came out to meet him, and said unto him, Come, and I will shew thee the man whom thou seekest. And when he came into her tent, behold, Sisera lay dead, and the nail was in his temples."*

2 Samuel 22:30-35, *"For by thee I have run through a troop: by my God have I leaped over a*

wall. **[31]** *As for God, his way is perfect; the word of the Lord is tried: he is a buckler to all them that trust in him.* **[32]** *For who is God, save the Lord? and who is a rock, save our God?* **[33] God is my strength and power: and he maketh my way perfect.** **[34] He maketh my feet like hinds' feet: and setteth me upon my high places.** **[35] He teacheth my hands to war; so that a bow of steel is broken by mine arms.**

Psalm 144:1-2, A Psalm of David, *"Blessed be the Lord my strength, which teacheth my hands to war, and my fingers to fight:* **[2]** *My goodness, and my fortress; my high tower, and my deliverer; my shield, and he in whom I trust; who subdueth my people under me."*

Joel 2:25-28, *"And I will restore to you the years that the locust hath eaten, the cankerworm, and the caterpiller, and the palmerworm, my great army which I sent among you.* **[26]** *And ye shall eat in plenty, and be satisfied, and praise the name of the Lord your God, that hath dealt wondrously with you: and my people shall never be ashamed.* **[27]** *And ye shall know that I am in the midst of Israel, and that I am the Lord your God, and none else: and my people shall never be ashamed.* **[28] And it shall come to pass afterward, that I will pour out my spirit upon all flesh; and your sons and your daughters shall** *prophesy, your old men shall dream dreams, your young men shall see visions:"*

PRAYERS ARROWS

- Lord forgive me for opening my territory to enemy invasion through sin, unbelief, ignorance; compromise; lack of discernment and spiritual carelessness.
- Lord teach my hands to war and my fingers to fight in the name of Jesus.
- I smash and bulldoze every obstacle on the way of my total recovery in the mighty name of Jesus.
- Lord, send me help from unexpected quarters in the name of Jesus.
- In the name of Jesus, I will surely recover all that pertain to my destiny 'without fail'
- My destiny will not be damaged beyond repair. My times O God are in your hand, deliver me from my enemies and from my persecutors in Jesus' name.
- Lord, let my enemies make the mistakes that will advance my cause in the name of Jesus.
- Lord, I shall not be a problem, I shall be a solution. Open my eyes to see those you have sent me to and to fulfil my assignment as helpers of their destinies.

- Father, throughout this year, make my ways prosperous in the precious name of Jesus
- Every lost ground to the enemy, I recover all now, I take it all back, by force in the name of Jesus.
- I retrieve every hidden gift and potential that will make me great in the name of Jesus.
- We recover every soul the enemy has held bound in this nation and in my family and command them to return to the Lord in the name of Jesus.
- Every prince of Persia, holding the manifestation of my miracle bound in the spirit, I command you to catch fire in the name of Jesus.
- I prophesy to all my inheritance that are hanging in the air, come back speedily into my life, in the name of Jesus.
- I decree concerning my Reuben, (Star, Glory, Destiny) live, and you shall not die, begin to shine and you shall not be vandalized, in the name of Jesus.
- Every power contending with my well of inheritance and well-being, scatter in the name of Jesus.
- Henceforth, men and women will come to the brightness of my star in the name of Jesus.
- Arise, o ye my blessing, glory, star, come to thy rest, and begin to shine in the name of Jesus.

I Will Recover All! (Operation Ziglag)

- I command the thunder of God to blast every lock used to lock up my miracles in the name of Jesus.

- I command all you gates shut against my possessions, lift up your heads now in the name of Jesus.

- As the earth opened its mouth to help the woman with the man-child, let the earth help me too, let the heavens assist me, let all creations join hands together to fight against my adversaries in the name of Jesus.

- I command all my glory, blessing and miracles in the camp of the enemy, receive wing and fly back into my life now in the name of Jesus.

- I command all robbers of my riches to vomit up all they have swallowed. Let God cast them out of their bellies.

- Thank you Father for my total recovery.

CHAPTER SEVEN

SHOOT THE ARROW OF DELIVERANCE

"Shoot...the arrow of the Lord's deliverance ...thou shall smite... till thou have consumed them" **2 Kings 13:17**

There is no limit to what God can do with your life. All the times, we are responsible for the limitation in our lives. God is willing to use what is in your hand to help you get what you need. You have to surrender and submit yourself and everything you think you have to God before God can bless you. God cannot increase what you do not release. *"Except a corn of wheat fall into the ground...it abideth alone..."* **John 12:24**.

In **2 Kings 13:14-19**, Elisha, the prophet was about to die. The king of Israel visited him. The prophet decided to give him a parting blessing which would have silenced his country's greatest enemy, Syria forever. Elisha told King Joash of Israel to shoot the arrows from his bow, as this would be the Arrows of Deliverance from the Syrians. He was also commanded to strike the ground with the arrows. He struck the ground three times and stopped. The prophet was annoyed with him. He said, if only he had not stopped, he would have received permanent deliverance from his enemies. I pray you will not stop taking it by force until you receive your permanent deliverance in Jesus' name.

We learn the following eternal lessons from the foregoing story:

1. We must trust and obey God and those who represent Him in our lives. His instruction may sound senseless, but God uses foolish things to confound the wise.

1 Corinthians 1:26-27, *"For ye see your calling, brethren, how that not many wise men after the flesh, not many mighty, not many noble, are called:* **[27]** *But God hath chosen the foolish things of the world to confound the wise; and God hath chosen the weak things of the world to confound the things which are mighty;"*

2. For true deliverance to occur, prayer must be persistent and persevering. You must pray without ceasing until your problem ceases to seize you. **Luke 18:1-8.**

3. Shooting an arrow continuously is a laborious exercise. Arrows are directed at specific targets. Success does not come easily; hard work and discipline would be required to accomplish great things. **Ecclesiastes 9:10,** *"Whatsoever thy hand findeth to do, do it with thy might; for there is no work, nor device, nor knowledge, nor wisdom, in the grave, whither thou goest."*

4. Underachievement comes as a result of underutilization of our potential. God will not ask you to do what you cannot possibly do. Elisha knew the king could do better. A man went to 98 banks before he could secure a much needed loan to start a business. The trouble with many believers today is that they give up too soon. I hear many say from time to time *"Pastor, I have prayed, I have fasted, I don't know what to do again!"* My answer is simple: *"Keep praying, keep fasting, keep praising God, help is not far away"*. Rachel cried: **"Give me children or I die!"** (**Genesis 30:1**). The way I interpreted her cry is this: *"I will not stop asking for children until I die"*. In the same way, if you truly desire a breakthrough, keep asking for it for as long as you have your breadth. George Muller, a legendry prayer warrior and man of faith prayed for 25 years for the salvation of the souls of four of his friends. He never gave up. In his lifetime, three of them surrendered their lives to Christ. The last one was an avowed atheist who had boasted that even if the God of George Muller came down, he will not surrender his life. On the day George Muller was being buried, this man broke down and gave his life to the God of George Muller just before the latter's body was lowered to the ground. I am sure the God of George came down and this man could not resist Him.

5. Half anything is bad. Thrice he struck instead of six times. Half education is bad; half-love is bad; half loyalty is bad, half commitment is bad; half obedience is bad; half concentration is bad; half giving is bad. What is worth doing at all is worth doing well. Whatsoever your hands finds to do, do it with all your might. You must double your efforts to do the right things right.

6. Do not try to control the Holy Spirit, let the Holy Spirit control you. I heard the testimony of a female top executive in a major Bank. She is a fervent and committed believer. One morning, she was corporately well dressed ready for the office. Shortly before she proceeded to her car, she recognised the voice of the Holy Spirit telling her to go and change her dress.

What the spirit was leading her to wear was ridiculous to say the least. In that dress she was to change to, she would have looked like a housewife going for a Saturday morning shopping in the local market. But she was too submissive to the Holy Spirit to disobey. She obeyed.

Later that day, as she sat in her office, three men walked into her office, after breaching all protocols. One of them looked intently at her and also at the picture in his hand. He concluded that she was not their target and all three of them, armed with automatic pistols left and walked away. Following the arrest of these men, they confessed that they had been hired to assassinate this woman, but the face on their picture did not match that of the one sitting on the desk that afternoon. The truth was that the way this lady dressed that day changed her look from that of a corporate executive to an ordinary local woman. Reward of yielding to the control of the Holy Spirit!

7.   If king Joash obeyed and did as he was expected to do, he would have reaped the blessings. Elisha was about to die. He was angry with the king because the king denied himself a permanent victory. When God gives you instruction and you obey, who benefits? When you sow, who reaps? When you pay your tithe, on whom will the windows of heaven be opened? When you pray hard for the peace of this nation, who gets the peace? **Jeremiah 29:7**. When you live Holy, who gains eternal life? **Isaiah 1:19; Job 36:11**.

TESTIMONY: Colonel Sanders was in his 60s. He had a recipe of fried chicken and he believed he could do good business with it. He knocked at the door of 1000 restaurants to sell his recipe. All except one turned him down. He could have given up at anytime up to the 999th attempt, but his dogged determination produced the world acclaimed Kentucky Fried Chicken (KFC) that is so popular today.

Richard Branson, a global icon and owner of Virgin conglomerate wrote recently: *"If you challenge yourself, you will grow. Your life will be positive. It's not always easy to* reach your goals but that's no reason to stop. Never say die. Say to yourself, 'I can do it. I'll keep trying until I win.'"

SCRIPTURES FOR MEDITATION AND PRAYER

2 Kings 13:14-19, *"Now Elisha was fallen sick of his sickness whereof he died. And Joash the king of Israel came down unto him, and wept over his face, and said, O my father, my father, the chariot of Israel, and the horsemen thereof. [15] And Elisha said unto him, Take bow and arrows. And he took unto him bow and arrows. [16] And he said to the king of Israel, Put thine hand upon the bow. And he put his hand upon it: and Elisha put his hands upon the king's hands. [17] And he said, Open the window eastward. And he opened it. Then Elisha said, Shoot. And he shot. And he said, The arrow of the Lord's deliverance, and the arrow of deliverance from Syria: for thou shalt smite the Syrians in Aphek, till thou have consumed them. [18] And he said, Take the arrows. And he took them. And he said unto the king of Israel, Smite upon the ground. And he smote thrice, and stayed. [19] And the man of God was wroth with him, and said, Thou shouldest have smitten five or six times; then hadst thou smitten Syria till thou hadst consumed it: whereas now thou shalt smite Syria but thrice."*

Luke 18:1, *"And he spake a parable unto them to this end, that men ought always to pray, and not to faint;"*

Acts 12:5, *"Peter therefore was kept in prison: but prayer was made without ceasing of the church unto God for him."*

Acts 1:8, *"But ye shall receive power, after that the Holy Ghost is come upon you: and ye shall be witnesses unto me both in Jerusalem, and in all Judaea, and in Samaria, and unto the uttermost part of the earth."*

2 Kings 4:1-7, *"Now there cried a certain woman of the wives of the sons of the prophets unto Elisha, saying, Thy servant my husband is dead; and thou knowest that thy servant did fear the Lord: and the creditor is come to take unto him my two sons to be bondmen. [2] And Elisha said unto her, What shall I do for thee? tell me, what hast thou in the house? And she said, Thine handmaid hath not any thing in the house, save a pot of oil. [3] Then he said, Go, borrow thee vessels abroad of all thy neighbours, even empty vessels; borrow not a few. [4] And when thou art come in, thou shalt shut the door upon thee and upon thy sons, and shalt pour out into all those vessels, and thou shalt set aside that which is full. [5] So she went from him, and shut the door upon her and upon her sons, who brought the vessels to her; and she poured out. [6] And it came to pass, when the*

vessels were full, that she said unto her son, Bring me yet a vessel. And he said unto her, There is not a vessel more. And the oil stayed. [7] *Then she came and told the man of God. And he said, Go, sell the oil, and pay thy debt, and live thou and thy children of the rest."*

Matthew 15:22-28, *"And, behold, a woman of Canaan came out of the same coasts, and cried unto him, saying, Have mercy on me, O Lord, thou Son of David; my daughter is grievously vexed with a devil.* [23] *But he answered her not a word. And his disciples came and besought him, saying, Send her away; for she crieth after us.* [24] *But he answered and said, I am not sent but unto the lost sheep of the house of Israel.* [25] *Then came she and worshipped him, saying, Lord, help me.* [26] *But he answered and said, It is not meet to take the children's bread, and to cast it to dogs.* [27] *And she said, Truth, Lord: yet the dogs eat of the crumbs which fall from their masters' table.* [28] *Then Jesus answered and said unto her, O woman, great is thy faith: be it unto thee even as thou wilt. And her daughter was made whole from that very hour."*

Jeremiah 29:11, *"For I know the thoughts that I think toward you, saith the Lord, thoughts of peace, and not of evil, to give you an expected end.*

PRAYER ARROWS

- Lord, I praise you. You are the Strength of Israel and the Arrow of my deliverance.

- I thank you Lord, for your thoughts towards me are good thoughts to give me a hope and a great future.

- Holy Spirit, fall upon me afresh in the mighty name of Jesus. *(Pray in tongues for a few minutes)*

- Lord, lay your supernatural hands upon my natural hands in the precious name of Jesus.

- Father, make me a weapon of war and a battle axe for your glory in Jesus' mighty name.

- Lord, open my eyes to see the gifts that are destined to make room for me in Jesus' name.

- Holy Spirit, anoint my tongue in the place of prayer and make me a sharp threshing instrument of war in the mighty name of Jesus.

- Let my imprisoned talents be released in the name of Jesus Christ.

- Father, deliver me from the spirit of frustration and hopelessness in the name of Jesus.

- Holy Spirit, anoint my life for unlimited exploits, empower me for unlimited greatness in the name of Jesus.

Shoot The Arrow Of Deliverance

- Lord, teach my hands to profit in the wonderful name of Jesus.
- Let every power attacking the peace, progress and prosperity of my family, my church and my city receive the arrow of deliverance in the name of Jesus.
- O earth; O earth, you must not co-operate with the enemy to afflict me in the name of Jesus.
- I decree that terrorists will not come into this city, *'nor shoot an arrow there, nor come before it with shield, nor cast a bank against it'* in the name of Jesus.
- Lord, defend my city against enemy attack, save her for your sake and for the sake of the believers dwelling in it in the precious name of Jesus.
- Let the arrow of the Lord's deliverance become an anti-missile to divert every arrow of the wicked fired at me and return it to the sender in the mighty name of Jesus.
- Hear my voice, O God in my prayer, preserve my life from the fear of the enemy. Shoot at them with an arrow; suddenly let them be wounded that seek after my life in the name of Jesus.
- I receive deliverance from the fear of the terror by night and from the arrow that flies at night in the powerful name of Jesus.

- In the name of Jesus, the sun shall not smite me by day neither the moon by night.
- Father, as arrows in the hands of a mighty man, let my quiver be full of godly, mighty children in Jesus' name.
- Lord, let your arrow go forth as lightning to destroy every altar of idolatry in this city and in my hometown in the name of Jesus.
- I fire the arrow of deliverance on the ground and I command every faulty foundation in my life to be uprooted right now in the name of Jesus. *(Do a prophetic action of firing arrows to the ground now)* Pray: By this arrow of deliverance, I smite sickness, be consumed; I smite poverty, be consumed; I smite barrenness, be consumed in the name of Jesus.
- I fire the arrows of deliverance against all spiritual amputators; physical destroyers and material robbers in the name of Jesus Christ.
- Father, send out your arrows and scatter the camp of my problems; send out your lightning and let them be discomfited in Jesus' mighty name.
- Blessed be the Lord my strength which teaches my hands to war and my fingers to fight. Happy and victorious I am because my God is the Lord.

CHAPTER EIGHT
BREAKING BARRIERS TO BREAKTHROUGHS

"One who breaks open the way will go up before them; they will break through the gate to go out. Their King will pass through before them, the Lord at their head". Micah 2:12 NIV.

Barriers are obstacles, obstructions, roadblocks that prevent the doing of something, the taking of something, the reaching of a destination or the achievement of a goal. Significant breakthroughs are not possible in life until one has removed certain barriers. This is why, at our church, Victory House, we speak of *"Breaking Through to your Breakthroughs"*.

In **Deuteronomy 1:2-7**, God spoke to the children of Israel. He told them they had dwelt long on the mountain of Horeb, that it was time to break every barrier and began to possess the lands that He promised them. God did not tell them they would have these lands on a platter of gold. They must contend in battle for the land. **Deuteronomy 2:24**, *"Rise ye up, take your journey, and pass over the river Arnon: behold, I have given into thine hand Sihon the Amorite, king of Heshbon, and his land:*

begin to possess it, and contend with him in battle."

Similarly, your time in the mountain of problems has expired. That mountain is a barrier to God's purpose for your life. It shall become a plain in the name of Jesus. **Zechariah 4:7**.

In **2 Samuel 23:15-17**, David longed for the delightsome and refreshing water of the well of Bethlehem. However, the garrison of the Philistines was a major barrier to fetching this water. Three of his mighty men of war volunteered to get him the water from this well of joy. They fought and 'broke through' the host of the Philistines and returned with breakthrough testimony. Are you longing for major breakthroughs? Every barrier on your way shall be broken in Jesus' name.

In **Daniel 10**, Daniel broke through to his breakthrough as he prayed and fasted for 21 days to dislodge the barriers erected by the prince of Persia against a royal postmaster of heaven (an angel) that was bringing his parcel of miracle. For every major achievement, there was a major barrier to break through. The size of your breakthrough would determine the size of the barrier you will have to break through.

A man needed his healing so desperately. The healer, our Lord Jesus Christ was in town preaching and the venue was filled to capacity. How would this man get to the feet of Jesus with such a major barrier? His helpers of destiny looked up, they broke through the roof. **Mark 2:4**. By the time the service was over, he went home healed. I command every barrier to your healing to break open in the name of Jesus.

Multitudes were the barriers to another woman's breakthrough. In **Mark 5:25-29**, she broke through the barrier and ended her twelve year affliction with a mighty testimony. You will break through every human barrier to your victory in the name of Jesus.

The principles that run through all these breakthrough stories are **Courage**; **Determination**; **Boldness**; **Faith**; **Perseverance**; **Persistence**; **Discipline**; **Commitment** and **Prevailing Prayer Power**. You too can be empowered by these virtues as you turn your focus to Jesus, wait on the Lord, pray persevering prayers and take steps of faith to break barriers to the breakthrough of the gospel, your loved ones and the entire human race.

TESTIMONY: As I wrote this chapter, the funeral rites of Ms. Rosa Parks was on. She made history as her body lie in honour in the Rotunda of the U.S. Capitol. Only very few American heroes enjoyed that privilege in America's history. Rosa Parks was the first woman to be so honoured, and a black woman for that matter. What was her testimony? She broke through the barrier of segregation and racism in Montgomery, Alabama in 1955 when she refused to give up her seat to a white passenger in a bus as required by the obnoxious segregation laws of the time. A committed Christian, Rosa believed she was created in the image of her God and no human being could claim superiority over her, certainly not on ground of colour. Her action was the beginning of the reversal of that *"Haman-like"* decree. The current American Secretary of State, Condoleeza Rice, in her tribute to Rosa said *"I think I can honestly say that without Ms. Parks, I would probably not be standing here today as U.S. Secretary of State"*.

Will you fight the good fight of faith, touching Heaven and affecting humanity so that by the time you finish the race and you are gone from this stage, someone will be saying the same thing about you?

SCRIPTURES FOR MEDITATION AND PRAYER

Deuteronomy 1:6-7, *"The Lord our God spake unto us in Horeb, saying, Ye have dwelt long enough in this mount: [7] Turn you, and take your journey, and go to the mount of the Amorites, and unto all the places nigh thereunto, in the plain, in the hills, and in the vale, and in the south, and by the sea side, to the land of the Canaanites, and unto Lebanon, unto the great river, the river Euphrates."*

Deuteronomy 2:24-25, *"Rise ye up, take your journey, and pass over the river Arnon: behold, I have given into thine hand Sihon the Amorite, king of Heshbon, and his land: begin to possess it, and contend with him in battle. [25] This day will I begin to put the dread of thee and the fear of thee upon the nations that are under the whole heaven, who shall hear report of thee, and shall tremble, and be in anguish because of thee."*

2 Samuel 23:15-17, *"And David longed, and said, Oh that one would give me drink of the water of the well of Bethlehem, which is by the gate! [16] And the three mighty men brake through the host of the Philistines, and drew water out of the well of Bethlehem, that was by the gate, and took it, and brought it to David: nevertheless he would not drink thereof, but poured it out unto the Lord. [17] And he said, Be it far from me, O Lord, that I should do this: is not this the blood of the men that went in jeopardy of their lives? therefore he would not drink it. These things did these three mighty men."*

Mark 2:4-7, *"And when they could not come nigh unto him for the press, they uncovered the roof where he was: and when they had broken it up, they let down the bed wherein the sick of the palsy lay. [5] When Jesus saw their faith, he said unto the sick of the palsy, Son, thy sins be forgiven thee. [6] But there were certain of the scribes sitting there, and reasoning in their hearts,* [7] *Why doth this man thus speak blasphemies? who can forgive sins but God only?"*

Psalm 24:7-10, *"Lift up your heads, O ye gates; and be ye lift up, ye everlasting doors; and the King of glory shall come in.* [8] *Who is this King of glory? The Lord strong and mighty, the Lord mighty in battle.* [9] *Lift up your heads, O ye gates; even lift them up, ye everlasting doors; and the King of glory shall come in.* [10] *Who is this King of glory? The Lord of hosts, he is the King of glory. Selah."*

Luke 1:37, *"For with God nothing shall be impossible."*

Daniel 10:12-13, *"Then said he unto me, Fear not, Daniel: for from the first day that thou didst set thine heart to understand, and to chasten thyself before thy God, thy words were heard, and I am come for thy words.* [13] *But the prince of the kingdom of Persia withstood me one and twenty days: but, lo, Michael, one of the chief princes, came to help me; and I remained there with the kings of Persia."*

PRAYER ARROWS:

- I praise you my Lord, the God that makes all things possible.

- I thank you Lord for all your past mercies and grace over me, my family, my city and my church.

- I lift up my voice, and I praise the Unchanging Changer who is the Greatest Barrier Breaker.

- Father, I confess and repent on behalf of my ancestors and I from the following sins committed against You: Rebellion; Murmuring; Unbelief and every form of disobedience.

- I renounce and denounce all self imposed and self inflicted barriers in my life.

- I declare that I have dwelt long enough upon the mountain of affliction, therefore let every such mountain become a plain right now in Jesus' name.

- I command all gates obstructing the glory of the Lord from coming upon this nation to lift up their heads in the name of Jesus.

- I command all barriers preventing the glory of the Lord from rising upon me to lift up their heads in the name of Jesus.

- I paralyze every prince of Persia assigned over my city in the mighty name of Jesus.

- Every power preventing the Royal Postmaster of Heaven from performing his assignment on my behalf, collapse now in the wonderful name of Jesus.

- Let all organized multitude against my breakthrough scatter now in Jesus' name.

- Let all organized confederacy against my breakthrough scatter now in the name of Jesus.

- Let all organized conspiracy against my breakthrough scatter now in the name of Jesus.

- I command every satanic garrison mounted against my well of Bethlehem to scatter now in the mighty name of Jesus.

- Father, raise helpers of destiny who will help me reach my goal of ultimate breakthrough this year in Jesus' name.

- I confess I have a goal of breakthrough to reach; my life will not waste in Jesus' name.

- Let fear turn to faith and let discouragement become courage for me in the name of Jesus.

- I receive the grace to begin to possess and contend in battle for my victory in the name of Jesus.

- This year, O Lord, let my breakthrough appear to all in the precious name of Jesus.

- Lord, go before me and make the rough places

- plain and the crooked places straight for me in Jesus' mighty name.
- I command the three-leafed gate of spiritual, physical and material breakthroughs to open to me in the name of Jesus.
- Lord, let my years of labour and toiling lead to ultimate breakthrough in Jesus' name.
- Father, let the gospel of Christ begin to enjoy astronomical and supernatural breakthrough in this city in the name of Jesus.
- Every barrier to the spread of the gospel in this nation, break into pieces in the name of Jesus.
- Let the powers, principalities, rulers of the darkness and spiritual wicked demons assigned over my city scatter in the name of Jesus.
- Oh you powers of darkness that say Jesus will not be Lord over this city, be slain in the name of Jesus.
- Oh you 'Jaazaniahs'. Oh you 'Pelatiahs' devising mischief and giving wicked counsel in this city, fall down and die in the name of Jesus.
- Every barrier to my Jericho inheritance, collapse in the name of Jesus Christ.
- As the light of this city, I prophesy to you wicked powers, this city shall not be your caldron; neither shall you be the flesh in the midst of her in the

- name of Jesus. You will fall by the sword of the word of God and the Lord will judge you in the border of this city in the name of Jesus Christ.

- Now Oh Lord, give the people of my city new hearts, put a new spirit within us; take away the stony heart out of our flesh and give us a heart of flesh in the merciful name of Jesus.

- Every barrier to the salvation of the souls of all my loved ones, I will see you collapse this year in the name of Jesus.

- Thank you Father, because your word for my breakthroughs shall no more be prolonged, they shall begin to come to pass from now on in the precious name of Jesus.

CHAPTER NINE
TAKE IT FORCEFULLY IN HIS NAME

"And whatsoever ye shall ask in my name, that will I do, that the Father may be glorified in the Son.
If ye shall ask any thing in my name, I will do it."
John 14:13-14

"For the weapons of our warfare are not carnal, but mighty through God to the pulling down of strongholds"
2 Corinthians 10:4.

Strongholds are the afflictions of life which contradict God's plans and purpose for our lives. Sickness, poverty, limitation, unbelief, impossibility are all strongholds which must not be tolerated in the believer's life.

God hates strongholds. It has pleased him to give us weapons to fight against them. The battle is called warfare. It is spiritual, it is not physical. Just as all blessings come from heavenly places in Christ, **Ephesians 1:3**, all problems come from heavenly places in satan. **Ephesians 6:12**. The mission of this hierarchy of evil powers is to afflict people with strongholds.

We must wage constant warfare to pull down strongholds. The weapons we use in this battle are described as not being carnal or fleshly. Rather, they are mighty through God for the destruction of these strongholds. You cannot successfully use any weapon against satan without due clearance from the Throne of Grace, which is our Supreme Headquarters.

One of the believers' most potent weapons is the name of Jesus. You can pull down strongholds through the name of Jesus and you can take back violently whatever the stronghold has taken from you through His name.

There are truths you must master about the name of Jesus Christ.

1. GOD HAS EMPOWERED THE NAME OF JESUS

Philippians 2:9-10, *"Wherefore God also hath highly exalted him, and given him a name which i s above every name:* [10] *That at the name of Jesus every knee should bow, of things in heaven, and things in earth, and things under the earth; God has made all things and all beings subject to the name of Jesus. Angels in heaven bow at His name; Men on earth bow at His name; Demons under the earth bow at His name. Dominion is in His name."*

2. GOD CAN AND WILL DO ANYTHING IN HIS NAME.

John 14:13-14, *"And whatsoever ye shall ask in my name, that will I do, that the Father may be glorified in the Son. [14] If ye shall ask any thing i n my name, I will do it."*

Note that whatsoever you ask must be in His Name! Asking in Jesus' name brings glory to God and God is committed to doing what will bring Him glory.

John 16:23, *"And in that day ye shall ask me nothing. Verily, verily, I say unto you, Whatsoever ye shall ask the Father in my name, he will give it you."*

Jesus encourages us ask in His name and we are to keep asking until our joy be full, in order words, until you receive satisfactory answer to your prayer.

John 16:24, *"Hitherto have ye asked nothing in my name: ask, and ye shall receive, that your joy may be full."*

3. BELIEVERS CAN AND WILL DO EXPLOITS IN HIS NAME

Jesus gave us the power of attorney to use His name and to enforce God's will on earth through his name. It is up to us to go ahead and do it. You do not need God to rebuke sickness; you are to rebuke it directly in the name of Jesus.

Mark 16:17, *"And these signs shall follow them that believe; In my name shall they cast out devils; they shall speak with new tongues;"*

4. THE EARLY CHURCH USED HIS NAME TO HEAL
Acts 3:6 ; Acts 16:18

The disciples put to test the mandate to do exploit with the name of Jesus and the name never failed them. In **Acts 3:16**, a man was lame from his mother's womb. Peter saw him and commanded him to rise up and walk in the name of Jesus. The affliction of that man ended there and then. Your affliction will end here and now in the name of Jesus. Similarly in **Acts 16:18**, Paul commanded an evil spirit to get out of a lady in the name of Jesus. The spirit obeyed at that very hour. These people were ordinary human beings like us, but they became extraordinary with the name of Jesus in their lips. Addressing those who were amazed by the miraculous healing of the lame man at Beautiful Gate, Peter told them the secret.

Acts 3:16, *"And his name through faith in his name hath made this man strong, whom ye see and know: yea, the faith which is by him hath* *given him this perfect soundness in the presence of you all."*

The name of Jesus will not work for just anybody. You must believe and have faith in his name, that is, you must be born again. The consequences of deploying the name of Jesus when you are not born again and living holy can be disastrous.

Acts 19:13-16, *"Then certain of the vagabond Jews, exorcists, took upon them to call over them which had evil spirits the name of the Lord Jesus, saying, We adjure you by Jesus whom Paul preacheth. [14] And there were seven sons of one Sceva, a Jew, and chief of the priests, which did so. [15] And the evil spirit answered and said, Jesus I know, and Paul I know; but who are ye? [16] And the man in whom the evil spirit was leaped on them, and overcame them, and prevailed against them, so that they fled out of that house naked and wounded."*

The name of Jesus is potent, protective and powerful. We are to use the name like a cheque book. The money is ever there. The healing is always there in His name.

In order for prayer to be effective and result-oriented, it must be said in the name of Jesus.

TESTIMONIES

ONE: Smith Wigglesworth testified of six men ministering to a man who was dying from tuberculosis. They prayed and nothing happened. One of them said *"There's one thing we've not done, let us go back and whisper the name of Jesus"*. They stood by the bed and kept repeating the name of Jesus over and over again. The presence of God began to fill the room and healing flowed into the dying man's body. He immediately arose, perfectly whole.

TWO: Pat Hayes was in a coma and on life support machine. She saw four angels of death coming to get her. She knew they were demonic spirits of death. Wondering what to do, she heard a still small voice "Just use my name". She began to call the name of Jesus even in her state, then, the brightest; the purest light moved over and took the place of these demons. The battle was won. She was taken off the life support the next day and went home healed.

SCRIPTURES FOR MEDITATION AND PRAYER

2 Corinthians 10:4, *"For the weapons of our warfare are not carnal, but mighty through God to the pulling down of strong holds;"*

Philippians 2:9-10, *"Wherefore God also hath highly exalted him, and given him a name which is above every name:* [10] *That at the name of Jesus every knee should bow, of things in heaven, and things in earth, and things under the earth;"*

John 14:13-14, *"And whatsoever ye shall ask in my name, that will I do, that the Father may be glorified in the Son.* [14] *If ye shall ask any thing in my name, I will do it."*

John 16:23, *"And in that day ye shall ask me nothing. Verily, verily, I say unto you, Whatsoever ye shall ask the Father in my name, he will give it you."*

Acts 3:6, *"Then Peter said, Silver and gold have I none; but such as I have give I thee: In the name of Jesus Christ of Nazareth rise up and walk."*

Acts 3:16, *"And his name through faith in his name hath made this man strong, whom ye see and know: yea, the faith which is by him hath given him this perfect soundness in the presence of you all."*

Acts 16:18, *"And this did she many days. But Paul, being grieved, turned and said to the spirit, I command thee in the name of Jesus Christ to come out of her. And he came out the same hour."*

Acts 19:13-16, *"Then certain of the vagabond Jews, exorcists, took upon them to call over them which had evil spirits the name of the Lord Jesus, saying, We adjure you by Jesus whom Paul preacheth.* [14] *And there were seven sons of one Sceva, a Jew, and chief of the priests, which did so.* [15] *And the evil* spirit answered and said, Jesus I know, and Paul I know; but who are ye? [16] And the man in whom the evil spirit was leaped on them, and overcame them, and prevailed against them, so that they fled out of that house naked and wounded."

Daniel 3:25, "He answered and said, Lo, I see four men loose, walking in the midst of the fire, and they have no hurt; and the form of the fourth is like the Son of God."

PRAYER ARROWS:

- Father, I thank you because you have given Jesus a name above all other names.

- I praise the highly exalted name of my Lord Jesus Christ for at the mention of His name, every knee must bow.

- I thank You Lord, for all those who believe in Jesus and in His name for they will not perish but will inherit eternal life. Thank you Lord for counting me worthy to be a partaker in this glorious inheritance.

- Thank you Lord for the name of Jesus that is so full of power of authority such that terror and fear consume principalities and powers at the mention of the name of Jesus.

Take It Forcefully In His Name

- I believe in the name of Jesus, therefore I have authority and power to enforce the will of God on earth and in my life through His precious name.

- Right now, I take authority over all powers of the enemy in the name of Jesus.

- I command demons behind any problem to be subject to me now through the name of Jesus.

- In the name of Jesus, I cast down every evil imagination exalting itself above the knowledge of Christ in my life and in my city.

- Lord, grant unto your Ministers boldness to speak your word and take authority using the name of Jesus.

- Father, stretch forth your hand to heal and let signs and wonders be done by the name of Your holy child Jesus.

- Father, let whatever will disqualify me from using the name of Jesus effectively be flushed out of my life in the name of Jesus.

- Let no demon be able to question my authority to use the Name of Jesus.

- I reject every form of unbelief in the name of Jesus Christ.

- I declare that greater is Jesus Christ that is in me than he that is in the world.

- Lord, expose every false prophet parading about in the name of Jesus.
- O Lord, let me not call the name of Jesus in vain!
- In the name of Jesus, I pull down every stronghold of sickness, disease, poverty and oppression in the name of Jesus.
- Let the name of Jesus protect me from sin, sickness and infirmities.
- Let the name of Jesus be enthroned over my city, community and nation.
- Let the name of Jesus become fire in my lips, consuming every demonic influence in the name of Jesus.
- Let the name of Jesus that rose up the lame man at Beautiful Gate begin to raise up every good thing that has become lame in my life and family.
- Lord Jesus, when I call your name in Prayer, answer me by fire!
- Father, in my sleep and in my waking moments, let the name of Jesus be a sharp, potent and powerful arrow in my lips.
- O Lord, in the day of trouble, let the name of Jesus defend me, let the name of the Son of God send me help in the name of Jesus.

Take It Forcefully In His Name

- Father, while others trust in chariots and in horses, let me remember the name of Jesus.

- The name of Jesus is a Strong Tower. Right now, I run into it and I am safe.

- Thank you Jesus. I will bless your name all the days of my life.

CHAPTER TEN

UPROOTING THE GATE OF THE ENEMY

"...and thy seed shall possess the gate of his enemies"
Genesis 22:17

Abraham's obedience provoked God's blessings upon his life afresh in Genesis 22. The Almighty assured Abraham that because of his obedience, He will not only bless him and his seed but his seed will also possess the gate of their enemies. To possess the gate of the enemy is to have power, dominion and victory over every barrier, entry point and obstacle that the enemy may bring on the way of Abraham's seed.

The good news is that every born again Christian is a seed of Abraham and therefore can rightly lay claim to this promise.

Galatians 3:29, *"And if ye be Christ's, then are ye Abraham's seed, and heirs according to the promise."*

However to possess the gate of the enemy involves a battle. You must do it by force because there are satanic overlords at the gate. You must overthrow them to overturn their gate. God loves it when his children take the battle to the gate of the enemy and He promised to give strength to those who do so.

Isaiah 28:5-6, *"In that day shall the Lord of hosts be for a crown of glory, and for a diadem of beauty, unto the residue of his people, [6] And for a spirit of judgment to him that sitteth in judgment, and for strength to them that turn the battle to the gate."*

There is an impressive story in the Bible of a seed of Abraham who appropriated this Abrahamic covenant by uprooting and possessing the gate of the enemy. You have many lessons to learn from his encounter before firing spiritual arrows of prayers to possess the gate of your enemy too.

Let us see the story of the man called Samson in **Judges 16:1-3**, *"Then went Samson to Gaza, and saw there an harlot, and went in unto her. [2] And it was told the Gazites, saying, Samson is come hither. And they compassed him in, and laid wait for him all night in the gate of the city, and were quiet all the night, saying, In the morning, when it is day, we shall kill him. [3] And Samson lay till midnight, and arose at midnight, and took the doors of the gate of the city, and the two posts, and went away with them, bar and all, and put them upon his shoulders, and carried them up to the top of an hill that is before Hebron."*

1. Samson went to Gaza and they told the Gazites that he was in town. A child of God must be careful where he allows his legs to carry him. You are under the constant surveillance of spiritual *'paparazis'*. They are watching every move you make. If you go into the territory of the enemy (sin), you will open yourself up to a devastating attack that only the grace and mercy of God can deliver you from.

2. *"And they compassed him in."* Instead of favour to surround this man, trouble surrounded him. Are you in that position? When everything seems to be against you. Everywhere you turn, there is one problem or the other you have to confront. David was once like that. He testified that the enemies surrounded him like bees, but in the name of the Lord he was sure of victory. **Psalm 18:4-5**; **Psalm 118:12**, *"They compassed me about like bees; they are quenched as the fire of thorns: for in the name of the Lord I will destroy them. This year, all the problems surrounding you will be destroyed in the name of the Lord Jesus Christ."*

3. The Gazites laid wait for him all night in the gate of the city. This shows how much the enemy can persevere at perpetrating destruction. They were not in a hurry at all. Satan can wait a whole century to destroy good things. When he left Jesus after the temptation, the Bible says he left him for a season. **Luke 4:13**. That is to say he was going to stage a comeback. Every plan of comeback of the enemy against you will fail woefully in the name of Jesus. The powers of darkness operate best under the cover of darkness; hence they were laying in wait all night. Every satanic night guards set against you will be frustrated in Jesus' name. Be careful when your star is shining. The enemies are waiting at the gate of the city of your breakthrough to attack and they don't care how long they wait to catch you! But in the name of the Lord, you will destroy them.

4. The Gazites were quiet all the night planning to kill Samson in the morning, when it is day. Can you see the counsel of wickedness? When God says *"weeping may endure in the night and in the morning cometh joy"* (**Psalm 30:5**), the devil is changing that to *"waiting may endure in the night but in the morning cometh sorrow"*. When witches and wizards have spent the night time to mutilate the destiny of their victims, in the morning you begin to hear all kinds of tragic incidents befallen such victims. An African proverb says that the witch cried last night and the child died in the morning, who does not know that it was the witch that killed the child. **Micah 2:1, *"Woe to them that devise iniquity, and work evil upon their beds! when the morning is light, they practise it, because it is in the power of their hand."*** I pray that the Lord will strip your enemies of all their powers to practice their evil on you and with everlasting shame and woe will He visit them in Jesus' name.

5. *"And Samson lay till midnight, and arose at midnight..."* We can see here a vital key to possessing the gate of the enemy. It is to be a midnight Christian. Look at Samson. He did not joke with his midnight. He arose at midnight. If he had slept through the night, he would have been a dead body by morning time. Many Christians are defeated because of spiritual slumbering. The devil has succeeded in tranquilizing many to a deep sleep, No night vigil, no night prayer and no night warfare. Where are the Pauls and Silases who will pray and sing praises at midnight until they possessed the prison doors and gates? (**Acts 16:15**) Where is the church that prayed without ceasing, through the night, until the city gates began to give way of its own accord to Peter? (**Acts 12:1-10**). It was while men slept that the enemy came and sow tares amongst the wheat. (**Matthew 13:25**). To take it by force, friend, you must arise at midnight!

6. Samson took the doors of the gate of the city, the posts, the bar and all, put them upon his shoulder and carried them up to the top of a hill. That speaks of tremendous supernatural power in fulfilment of God's promise to give strength to them that takes the battle to the gate. Divine help to do this exploit would not have come if he had slept through the night. Samson uprooted and possessed the gate of his enemies. Those who need divine intervention must take steps of faith. He went to the top of a hill. That is where you are destined for. You will ascend the top this year in Jesus' name. You shall be blessed, you shall be lifted and it shall be well with you.

7. The final point from this story is to ask the question: where were all the satanic overlords who laid in waiting for Samson when Samson was uprooting the doors, the bars and the posts of the gate and carting them away? My answer is that the Lord sent them to a deep sleep. (**1 Samuel 26:12**). When you pray fervent, persistent and violent prayers, the Lord will send your enemies to a deep sleep and you will enjoy a safe passage to your breakthrough. Why don't you arise and dedicate the next three nights to a personal night vigil to do spiritual warfare to uproot every evil gate of problems around you and your family?

TESTIMONY: A Chinese Christian, named Bro. Yun was arrested and persecuted for his faith in China. He was thrown into jail and the authorities were determined to forget him in prison for life. While in the prison, Bro. Yun prayed, fasted and praised God day and night. Many prisoners were saved through his prayers and witness. Then one day, following a long period of praying and fasting, He had a witness in his spirit that it was time for his supernatural release. Bro. Yun took steps of faith to get out of the prison. He did not break any prison door or had any external human help. The prison doors and gates simply began to open for him one after the other, of their own accord. All the prison keepers were there while Bro. Yun made his way towards the prison exit but none seemed to see him. (The Lord blinded all of them to His servant). By the time Bro. Yun got outside the prison, a cab was waiting to pick him up. He entered the cab and the cab man drove him through the town and parked in front of the house of some Christians. He told Bro. Yun to alight from the cab without asking for any payment from him and drove off. (Could this be an angel of the Lord?). Bro. Yun walked into the hands of his Christian friends who told him that the Lord showed them the previous night as they were praying that He will set him free from the prison.

In the same way, the Lord will set you free from every prison of the enemy in the name of Jesus.

SCRIPTURES FOR MEDITATION AND PRAYER

Judges 16:2-3, *"And it was told the Gazites, saying, Samson is come hither. And they compassed him in, and laid wait for him all night in the gate of the city, and were quiet all the night, saying, In the morning, when it is day, we shall kill him. [3] And Samson lay till midnight, and arose at midnight, and took the doors of the gate of the city, and the two posts, and went away with them, bar and all, and put them upon his shoulders, and carried them up to the top of an hill that is before Hebron."*

Genesis 22:17, *"That in blessing I will bless thee, and in multiplying I will multiply thy seed as the stars of the heaven, and as the sand which is upon the sea shore; and thy seed shall possess the gate of his enemies;"*

Galatians 3:29, *"And if ye be Christ's, then are ye Abraham's seed, and heirs according to the promise."*

Isaiah 28:5-6, *"In that day shall the Lord of hosts be for a crown of glory, and for a diadem of beauty, unto the residue of his people, [6] And for a spirit of judgment to him that sitteth in judgment, and for strength to them that turn the battle to the gate."*

Psalm 18:4-5, *"The sorrows of death compassed me, and the floods of ungodly men made me afraid. [5] The sorrows of hell compassed me about: the snares of death prevented me."*

Psalm 118:12, *"They compassed me about like bees; they are quenched as the fire of thorns: for in the name of the Lord I will destroy them."*

Psalm 30:5, *"For his anger endureth but a moment; in his favour is life: weeping may endure for a night, but joy cometh in the morning."*

Micah 2:1, *"Woe to them that devise iniquity, and work evil upon their beds! when the morning is light, they practise it, because it is in the power of their hand."*

Acts 16:25, *"And at midnight Paul and Silas prayed, and sang praises unto God: and the prisoners heard them."*

1 Samuel 26:12, *"So David took the spear and the cruse of water from Saul's bolster; and they gat them away, and no man saw it, nor knew it, neither awaked: for they were all asleep; because a deep sleep from the Lord was fallen upon them."*

PRAYER ARROWS

- I praise you my Lord the Man of War.
- I bless the name of the Lord my God, who teaches my hands to war and my fingers to fight.
- Lord, I repent before you today of all my acts of spiritual carelessness and insensitivity to your Holy Spirit in my life.
- Father, I am sorry for giving the enemy an inroad into my life through my sin of walking into the wrong places and doing the wrong things.
- I receive total forgiveness through the precious blood of Jesus Christ.
- I confess that I am a seed of Abraham, therefore, I am covenanted to possess the gate of the enemy in the name of Jesus.

Uprooting The Gate Of The Enemy

- As I take the battle to the gate of the enemy, I receive divine strength for victory in the name of Jesus.

- Let every power monitoring my movements to do me evil receive the arrow of fire in the powerful name of Jesus.

- I command every satanic monitoring gadget set up for my sake to catch fire and be burnt to ashes now in the mighty name of Jesus.

- I decree woe and destruction unto the camp of wicked powers who devices evil in the night and plot to execute mischief in the morning in the name of Jesus.

- I command every spiritual mines and traps set up for me to be incapacitated in the name of Jesus.

- Let every laying in wait for me be of no effect whatsoever in the name of Jesus Christ.

- O Lord, frustrate the tokens of liars and make all diviners and enchanters mad for my sake in the name of Jesus.

- Holy Spirit alarm, wake me up, keep me alert and don't let me slumber away while the enemy enjoys a field day over my destiny.

- O Lord, send my adversaries to a deep sleep until I have escaped to victory in the name of Jesus.

- Every ear listening quietly to my footsteps to breakthrough with intent to derail me, receive deafness now in Jesus' name.
- Every eye, watching my ascent to the top with intent to pull me down, receive blindness now in the name of Jesus.
- I shall not sleep the sleep of death in the merciful name of Jesus.
- Holy Ghost, give me spiritual sensitivity during the daytime and give me spiritual alertness during the night time in the name of Jesus, the Keeper of Israel who neither sleep nor slumber.
- O thou sun, you will not smite me and my loved ones by day. O thou moon, you will not smite me and my loved ones by night in Jesus' name.
- O Lord, you are the consuming fire, consume all satanic overlords hired against me in the name of Jesus Christ.
- In the name of Jesus, I uproot every gate of death, failure, sickness, poverty, stagnation and trouble erected for my sake in the name of Jesus.
- Every gate erected against the gospel of our Lord Jesus Christ in this city, be uprooted by fire in Jesus' name.
- Lord, make me a mountain climber and let the enemy see me on top of the hill this year.

Uprooting The Gate Of The Enemy

- Thou angels of lifting, go forth on assignment for my sake this year in Jesus' name.

- Let the devices of the wicked be disappointed and let them not be able to perform their enterprise in the name of Jesus.

- Let every plot to sow tares amongst the wheat of my destiny be frustrated in the name of Jesus Christ.

- I receive the anointing and the supernatural strength to possess the gate of the enemy in Jesus' name.

- I command every door and every gate that have shut good things away from me to begin to open of their own accord right now in Jesus' mighty name.

- Let the fire of thorns begin to quench every problem that has compassed me as bees in the mighty name of Jesus.

- This year, I run through the troops, I break the bow of steel and I overcome all my adversaries in the name of Jesus.

- This year, let the city gate of my ultimate breakthrough begin to open of its own accord in the powerful name of Jesus Christ.

- Father, catapult me from Gaza, lift me up to the top of the hill that is before Hebron in the name of Jesus Christ.

- Let every plant which my heavenly Father had not planted in my life be uprooted right now in the name of Jesus.

- Thank you my Father, for giving me this victory over every gate, bar and post of the enemy in Jesus' precious and wonderful name.

APPENDIX

Other Books by the Author

1) **NONE SHALL BE BARREN** *(The Testimony of A Couple's trials and triumphs over barrenness)* This book is now a popular movie **"Agan"** (subtitled in English)

2) **GOLIATH KILLING PRAYERS** *(How to Overcome Every Giant of Your Life)*

3) **POWER TO BREAK THROUGH TO YOUR BREAKTHROUGHS** *(A 21-day prayer strategy for all round victory)*

4) **52 INDISPENSABLE PRAYERS** *(Prayer Nuggets to Renew your body; Refresh your Soul and Refire your Spirit)*

Take It by Force! *- How To Possess Your Possessions*

I would love to hear from you. Please send your comments, testimonies and prayer requests to me in care of the address below. Thank you.

RCCG VICTORY HOUSE

5 Congreve Street, Old Kent Road

London. SE17 1TJ

Tel: +44 207 252 7522

E-mail: lekesanusi@rccgvictoryhouse.com

Or leke@sanusi.fsnet.co.uk